INCREDIBLE BASEBALL FEATS

brings you astonishing events from all aspects
of the game—the majors, the minors, and
amateurs!

Here are answers to such questions as—
• Who pitched the most perfect innings in
baseball history? • Who is the oldest man ever
to pitch a no-hitter? • What's the record time
for rounding the bases? • What team scored
after the last out? • How come 38 homers
were enough to win a batter *four* major-league
home-run titles? • Who hit 72 home runs in
one season?

And many more incredible feats of Pitching,
Hitting, and Fielding—team and individual,
young and old—and downright amazing!

Incredible Baseball Feats

By Jim Benagh

tempo
books

GROSSET & DUNLAP
Publishers   New York

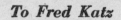

To Fred Katz

Contents

MISCELLANEOUS

Foreword

A very fine sportswriter named Leonard Koppett once brought up an interesting point in his *Sporting News* column about the perishability of startling records even in a sport like baseball, where figures and events are meticulously cared for. He noted that after a rash of unassisted triple plays—there were five in the major leagues during a four-year stretch in the 1920s—some newspapers began ho-humming the remarkable feat. In fact, Koppett added, the fifth of those unassisted triple plays came exactly one day after the fourth one, so a major New York newspaper saw fit to give it only one obscure sentence of recognition. It was 40 years before another unassisted triple play was made at the major-league level.

"There's simply too much going on in sports for any immortal event to retain its immortality," wrote Koppett. Perhaps he's correct, and if so it's

1

a shame. I've always found sports records, and particularly the incredible feats that sometimes aren't records at all in the official sense, worth recalling. They give sports an added dimension in their combat with the routine of daily life.

Thus, *Incredible Baseball Feats*, like its companion books *Incredible Football Feats* and *Incredible Basketball Feats*, is an attempt to relive some of the remarkable happenings of baseball.

There was no exact formula for selecting the entries for *Incredible Baseball Feats* except, of course, that they fit the category "incredible." I looked particularly for some of the non-record happenings, such as the strange strikeout spell rookie pitcher Hub Pruett held over Babe Ruth. But I also dug into minor-league baseball archives, because some of the most incredible feats have been lost with the diminishing importance of the baseball farm systems.

The reader should note that many very important feats may have been left out of this book—such as DiMaggio's 56-game hitting streak—because so much has been written about them, not because I underestimate their importance. I felt the rare and forgotten feats would be more interesting to the reader of this book.

To research the book, I turned to many sources and sportswriters. It would be difficult to list all of them here. But I am particularly indebted to the Baseball Hall of Fame in Cooperstown, New

York, which has put together what must be the best library on any sport ever. My sincere thanks go to Hall of Fame librarian Jack Redding and historian Cliff Kachline and other members of their staff. I also owe special thanks to Bill Madden of United Press International, author Larry Bortstein, and sportswriter Art Berke, and many of the athletes included herein, who gave me additional information about their own feats.

It was impossible to list all of the feats I wanted to; nevertheless, I would appreciate hearing from readers about feats that could be included in later editions of *Incredible Baseball Feats*. Please write (Post Office Box 1113, Englewood Cliffs, N.J. 07632) should you have a favorite one worth including.

JIM BENAGH

January, 1975

STRONG ARMS

The Pitcher Who Struck Out Babe Ruth

Baseball has a term for a pitcher who's got a batter's number. It's called a "collar."

Babe Ruth, the remarkable workhorse of the New York Yankees, rarely was stopped repeatedly by any pitcher during his dazzling 22-year career— and if he was, he wasn't for long. A .343 lifetime hitter with those famous 714 home runs, Ruth could hit his way out of any adverse situation.

But there was one season when Ruth was collared by a pitcher. It happened in 1922. Babe's conqueror turned out to be a twenty-one-year-old rookie who bore the nickname "Shucks."

Hub (Shucks) Pruett was a little 165-pounder for the St. Louis Browns, who were to give the Yankees a run for the American League pennant in 1922. Baseball was secondary to Pruett. A graduate of the University of Missouri, he was more intent on working his way through medical school than collaring future Hall of Famers.

Pruett wasn't any more awed by his own baseball talents than he was by those of famous opponents like Ruth. As a youth, he remembered that his sandlot friends made him pitch because he couldn't throw straight from other positions. At the University of Missouri, he had a little curve and a screwball and not much more, in his own estimation. "I didn't think I could fool major leaguers," he said years later. But he needed the money, so he tried.

What Hub Pruett did to Ruth in 1922 has grown in legend over the years. The *Sporting News,* baseball's generally reliable "bible," once ran an article that mentioned Pruett fanning Ruth 13 straight times and giving him only one hit in 19 times at bat during the heated pennant race between St. Louis and the Yankees in 1922. That would have been some accomplishment for a pitcher who posted only a 7-7 record for his first big-league season.

Even Pruett wasn't that good.

But he was good enough.

Subsequent research by sportswriter Robert Creamer for his magnificent biography *Babe: The Legend Comes to Life* points out that between May and September of 1922, Shucks Pruett struck out Ruth 10 times in the 16 times the mighty Yankee confronted him. Since Pruett walked

Ruth three times, that was 10 "K's" in 13 official at-bats.

Of the first 12 times Ruth swung against the Brown upstart, over a course of five games, the Babe struck out nine times and once grounded out meekly to the pitcher. The ground-out in the fourth game was the closest Ruth had come to getting a piece of the ball in four months against his newly found nemesis. In two other plate appearances, Pruett walked Ruth.

Here's how Pruett did it:

May 22: In a four-inning relief stint, Pruett struck out Ruth and walked him once. Ruth had homered against the Browns earlier in the game.

June 10: Again in relief, Pruett fanned Ruth the only time they faced each other.

June 12: Making his first start against the Yankees, Pruett struck out Ruth three times and walked him once—and got credit for winning the game, though he lasted only six innings.

July 12: Again, Pruett set Ruth down swinging three times and got him the last time with the bases loaded to preserve a 7-4 victory for the Browns. In another confrontation that day, Ruth got a piece of the ball and dribbled it back to Pruett for an infield out.

August 25: Pruett was still suffering from a sore arm that had cost him an opportunity to meet Ruth for a second time in July. But when

Ruth came to bat with the bases loaded, he pitched anyway and, naturally, struck him out.

September 17: By now, the pennant race was hot and the fans were siding with the amazing rookie phenom who had struck out Ruth in nine of 10 official at-bats. Pruett revved up that crowd even more when, after walking Ruth in the first inning, he struck him out in the third. Ruth finally broke the spell in the fifth inning with one of his towering home runs. Later in the game, which the Browns won by a 5-1 score, Ruth also singled.

They didn't meet again until 1923.

For the season, Ruth had batted only .158 against a good though hardly sensational rookie. A man who homered in one out of every 8.5 at-bats during his fabled career managed just one homer in 13 at-bats against a heretofore unknown.

Ruth hit only .315 and 35 homers in 1922—well below his usual norms. But that should not detract from Pruett's accomplishments.

The following season, when Ruth got back into the groove (batting .393 and smacking a league-leading 41 homers), Pruett again began to harass him. Pruett struck him out three times in their first meeting, though he gave up a walk and a homer in the same contest.

Thus Pruett brought his remarkable string to 13 strikeouts in 17 official at-bats by Ruth.

Shucks Pruett was often asked how a raw rookie like himself could "collar" the most famous slugger in baseball history. He said he had no secret and didn't pitch any differently than he did to other players, who gave him more than his share of problems. He had a lefthanded version of Christy Mathewson's strange fadeaway pitch, and that was the particular pitch that befuddled Ruth in crucial situations. It fell away from the plate when it neared the home-run-hunting slugger.

"I suppose I just didn't have the mental hazard," mused Pruett in later years. "I suppose the reason for that was that I wasn't a rabid fan as a kid. Big names didn't mean as much. I wanted to be a doctor."

Pruett made a name for himself that first season. Though he was no raving success, except against Ruth, he did strike out 70 men in slightly less than 120 innings and was a good enough hurler to help the Browns make a run for the pennant.

After his first matchup with Ruth in 1923, however, he held no more spell over the Yankee and struck him out only one more time. For 1923 and 1924, Pruett won only seven games for the Browns and was phased out of the American League. He managed to get four more seasons of play in the National League between 1927 and 1932, then retired from the game with a mediocre 29-48 record.

But during his undistinguished major-league career, he earned his medical degree, and became a practicing physician in St. Louis. He wasn't a bragger, but he liked to talk about the old days when Babe Ruth put him through medical school. It was a kindness Ruth gave to no other pitcher during his famed career.

The Righthander Who Struck Out 27 Men in a Game

To strike out five of six batters is an accomplishment that any pitcher would like. But to strike out five of *every* six men you face is something pitchers don't even bother to fantasize about.

Yet one man achieved that feat—and a lot of other strikeout feats—during his short stay in the minor leagues during the 1952 season.

Until May 13 of that year, Ron Necciai's name was known only for its difficult pronunciation *Netch*-eye)—and known only within the vast Pittsburgh Pirate farm system. The Pirates' brilliant general manager, Branch Rickey, had tried to launch the reorganization of the downtrodden Pirates by rounding up as many strong-armed American youths as he could. Rickey was dealing in numbers; Necciai, a nineteen-year-old ex-football star from Monongahela, Pa., was just one of them.

Necciai was shipped out to an Appalachian League team of Bristol, which represented the twin cities of that name in Virginia and Tennessee. Bristol was Class D baseball, as low as you can get, but a good starting point for unseasoned teenagers just out of high school.

When Necciai reported, he found himself among a lot of strong arms that the Rickey network had discovered. Among his teammates were two pitchers named Bill Bell (who would record 194 strikeouts in 112 innings that year) and Frank Ramsey (180 strikeouts in 194 innings).

After a couple of warmup games, however, none of the fastball pitchers could match Necciai.

A crowd of 1,853 gathered at Bristol, Va., on May 13 to watch the local team play Welch, W. Va., in a regular-season contest. What they saw was beyond belief.

Necciai, a sturdy righthander, struck out the side in the first inning. He struck out the first man to face him in the second. Then the Welch team's leftfielder got a piece of the ball but grounded out, shortstop to first base. Necciai fanned the last batter of the inning.

And the next three.

And the next three.

And so on.

Going into the ninth inning, the amazing left-hander had struck out 23 batters. Only that ground-ball out in the second inning prevented him from recording 24 out of a possible 24 strikeouts in the first eight innings.

In the top of the ninth inning, Necciai struck out two more men to bring his game total to 25—matching the all-time organized (professional) baseball record for one game.

Along with the incredible strikeout string, Necciai had a no-hit game going. The only batters to reach base were one whom Necciai hit with a pitch and another whom he walked. Most of his teammates could have taken the night off. But not the catcher.

Behind the plate that night was Harry Dunlop, who was earning his salary that season trying to control Branch Rickey's whiff kids. He had done a marvelous job handling Necciai throughout the first eight innings.

But with two outs in the ninth, Dunlop dropped a third strike. Before he could recover the ball, Welch's speedy centerfielder Bobby Hammond scampered to first base.

By baseball scoring rules, the pitcher still gets credit for a strikeout if the catcher muffs the third strike. The catcher is given an error for the play. Thus, it's possible to have infinite strikeouts in a game—theoretically.

But 26 for the night is a startling performance, too. And that's just what Necciai had as he took the mound to face another Welch batter. He then proceeded to strike out one more and bring his total to 27—a record no one has come close to matching in professional baseball. Almost as impressive was the fact that 10 of those opponents had watched Necciai's fastball whiz by them without taking the bats off their shoulders. He was that fast that night.

Necciai naturally became the talk of the baseball world right after his astounding performance. Branch Rickey dispatched his son, Branch Jr., to Bristol to keep an eye on the arm. National League President Warren Giles wired Necciai to tell him, "I hope it won't be long before you're striking out American League batters in the All-Star Game." And potential ticket buyers in the little minor-league community anxiously awaited Necciai's next start.

Was his performance a fluke?

Hardly.

Necciai didn't start again until May 21, eight nights later. But against the Kingsport, Tenn. team, he fanned a grand total of 24 batters in a nine-inning game. A crowd of more than 5,000 cheered him on.

In his next two starts, Necciai continued to daze the youthful opponents who made up Class

D rosters. He recorded 20 and then 19 strike-outs. That brought his total to 90 in four full games. Combined with the strikeouts he had in parts of two other games for Bristol, Necciai now had a total of 109 strikeouts in 42 ⅔ innings. In addition, he had a 4-0 record, and had given up only two earned runs during his stay at Bristol. His control had been pretty good, too; his slate showed only 20 walks and 10 hits in that span. He was not yet 20 years old.

Meanwhile, he had made believers out of Rickey and Co. The Pirates advanced him to their Bur-lington (North Carolina) team for a brief stay in better competition—and then up to the majors at the end of the season.

Necciai didn't awe the big leaguers with his fastball. But the Pirates were a miserable last place team, 54½ games behind the league leaders, and they thus offered little support for a young pitcher just off the sandlots of nearby Monon-gahela. Necciai pitched 54⅔ innings in 12 games and struck out 31 batters. He won one of seven decisions.

Ulcers, a sore arm and other physical problems caused by the strain on his lanky 6-foot, 5-inch, 185-pound body curtailed Necciai's develop-ment. He toiled in the minors for some time after 1952, then faded out of the baseball picture. He never did reach the majors again.

Necciai's 27-strikeout Game

Welch	AB	R	H	O	A	E
Germano, ss	3	0	0	3	1	1
†Whitehead	1	0	0	0	0	0
Shelton, 1b	2	0	0	4	1	2
‡Uram	1	0	0	0	0	0
Hammond, cf	4	0	0	1	0	0
Kendrick, lf	4	0	0	2	0	0
Ganung, rf	2	0	0	0	0	1
Barry, c	3	0	0	10	0	0
Giel, 3b	3	0	0	2	2	0
Laney, 2b	3	0	0	1	1	0
Crammer, p	0	0	0	0	0	0
Moore, p	1	0	0	1	1	0
*Ferger	1	0	0	0	0	0
Chilton, p	1	0	0	0	0	2
Totals	29	0	0	24	6	6

Bristol	AB	R	H	O	A	E
Lipstas, cf	2	1	0	0	0	0
Filiatrault, 1b	4	2	1	2	0	0
Chrisley, lf	3	0	0	0	0	0
Dunlop, c	3	0	1	25	1	1
Novotniak, 3b	2	1	0	0	0	0
Greenhill, rf	5	0	1	0	0	0
Burch, 2b	4	1	0	0	0	0
DeVeau, ss	5	1	2	0	1	1
Necciai, p	4	1	1	0	0	1
Totals	32	7	6	27	2	3

```
Welch ............. 0  0  0   0  0  0   0  0  0—0
Bristol ........... 1  1  0   1  1  2   1  0  —7
```

*Struck out for Moore in sixth inning. †Reached first base
on error for Germano in ninth inning. ‡Struck out for Shelton
in ninth inning. Runs batted in—Filiatrault, Dunlop 2, Novot-
niak 2. Two-base hits—Dunlop, DeVeau 2. Sacrifice—Burch.
Left on bases—Welch 4, Bristol 14. Bases on balls—Off Necciai
1, off Crammer 4, off Moore 6, off Chilton 1. Struck out—By
Necciai 27, by Moore 4, by Chilton 5. Pitching records—Off
Crammer 0 hits in ⅓ inning, off Moore 3 hits in 4⅔ innings, off

The nickname for Bristol's team, since it represented two cities, appropriately was the Twins. And in 1952, Ron Necciai was operating as only part of a tandem of record breakers.

His teammate, Bill Bell, was also a strikeout whiz. And during the month of May that year, Bell teamed with Necciai to perform perhaps the most unusual series of games ever staged by two minor-league pitchers. On May 13, Necciai had his 27-strikeout no-hitter. Then on May 22, Bell went out and pitched a no-hitter against Kingsport only one night after Necciai had fanned 24 of the Kingsport batters.

It was strange as no-hitters go, because Bell let 11 batters get on base via walks. Two others got on base via errors. Still, Bell hung in there, striking out 17 batters, and collected a 1-0 run victory when he scored himself.

Necciai fanned 20 batters in his next start and Bell, not to be one-upped, went out on May 26 and pitched his second consecutive no-hitter, beating Bluefield, W. Va., 4-0.

Enough was not enough, though. With Necciai in the majors in Pittsburgh, Bell went out and pitched a third no-hitter for Bristol on August 25, again setting down Bluefield by the same 4-0 score.

Chilton 3 hits in 3 innings. Hit by pitcher—By Necciai 1 (Shelton). Losing pitcher—Crammer. Umpires—Sprague and Weiner. Time of game—2:23. Attendance—1,853.

What could Bristol then do for an encore?

On August 26, the night after Bell's third no hitter, Bristol's Frank Ramsey blanked Bluefield again, 1-0—in a no-hitter!

The Fastest Throws Ever Recorded

When a pitcher strikes out 19, 9 and 19 men in three consecutive games, it's quite clear that he has something on the ball. For Nolan Ryan, the record-breaking righthander of the California Angels, it was speed. Legitimate 100 mile-an-hour speed. In fact, when Ryan's fastball was timed during the final game of that marvelous stretch in 1974, two of his pitches were clocked at 100.9 mph each—the fastest throws ever recorded. They broke the long-lasting mark of 98.6, set by Bob (Rapid Robert) Feller in 1946.

In fairness to old-time pitchers such as Walter

Incredible Baseball Feats

Johnson, the post-World War II mound whizzes have had the benefit of electronic timing devices. There just wasn't any way of clocking the speedball kings before Feller had U. S. Army equipment time his warmup pitches at Griffith Stadium, Washington, D.C., in August of 1946.

But Ryan's dazzling three-year record with over 1,000 strikeouts—including a record 383 in 1973—supports his claim to the speed king title. No one else has ever topped 100 under electronic surveillance, and he did it more than once and during game conditions.

Ryan's two 100.9-mph pitches were posted exactly 28 years to the day after Feller turned in his 98.6. Ryan first did it when he faced Detroit Tiger leadoff man Ron LeFlore in the first inning of an August 20, 1974, game. He matched that speed later in the game en route to a 19-strikeout, 11-inning game—which he lost, 1-0.

Two and a half weeks later, Ryan was timed again and nearly equaled his record by throwing the ball 100.8 mph. And that was in the ninth inning as he pitched a tough, tight game against the Chicago White Sox. Actually, Ryan had been tested in five pregame warmup pitches but could do no better than 88.5 mph.

The Ryan tests were done with sophisticated equipment provided by a group of Rockwell International scientists. They used an infra-red radar device which was placed in the Angel press box.

The record didn't set too well with Ryan, though. He expressed indifference to being clocked —the Angels had made a major publicity drive for the White Sox game—under game conditions.

"I don't like to do it because it takes too much away from my concentration," said Ryan after the game. "Any time you do something like that you've got to be prepared for the worst and I'm glad to get it over."

Among the ten fastest pitchers with official clockings are five (Don Drysdale, Steve Barber, Herb Score, Ryne Duren, and Sandy Koufax) who made it on the same day. In 1960, they and Bob Turley took part in a test arranged by a national magazine during spring training. All were clocked over 90 mph. Turley, who finished last in the test, had joined the "90-mph Club" in 1958, when he was timed at 94.2.

Perhaps the most interesting member of the 90-mph group is Steve Dalkowski, a one-time farmhand of the Baltimore Orioles. He was taken out to Aberdeen Proving Grounds, the military post near Baltimore, and was clocked at 93.5 in 1958. He may have been even faster but he wasn't pitching from a mound (as Feller and others had done), and the wild-throwing speedballer had to throw for 40 minutes in warmups just trying to find the range of the testing equipment. There are those who claim Dalkowski may have been the fastest ever. But his lack of control kept him out of the major leagues. His strikeout records as a professional are awesome: 1,396 in 995 innings during nine years in the minor leagues. But then again, his walks were awesome, too: 1,345. As a high-school pitcher he once walked 8 men in a no-hit performance. As a pro, he both struck out and walked 21 men in separate outings. He dropped out of pro ball in 1966 at age twenty-six. His 46-80 won-loss record and 5.67 earned run average just weren't the right stuff to go along with his fastball.

The 90-mph Club

	Name (Team)	Speed	Year	Threw
1.	Nolan Ryan (California Angels)	100.9	1974	R
2.	Bob Feller (Cleveland Indians)	98.6	1946	R
3.	Steve Barber (Baltimore Orioles)	95.5	1960	L
4.	Don Drysdale (Los Angeles Dodgers)	95.3	1960	R
5.	Atley Donald (New York Yankees)	94.7	1939	R
6.	Bob Turley (New York Yankees)	94.2	1958	R
7.	Steve Dalkowski (minor leagues)	93.5	1958	L
8.	Sandy Koufax (Los Angeles Dodgers)	93.2	1960	L
9.	Ryne Duren (New York Yankees)	91.1	1960	R
10.	Herb Score (Chicago White Sox)	91.0	1960	L

He Struck Out Six All-Stars in Two Innings

The crowd of 50,000 at big-league baseball's second annual All-Star Game in 1934 was in for an early disappointment. The game was being played at the Polo Grounds in New York City and the host team's favorite hero, pitcher Carl Hubbell of the New York Giants, was in deep trouble. Charlie Gehringer of the Detroit Tigers had led off with a single and Heinie Manush of the Washington Senators drew a walk. There were no outs in the first inning.

The walk is what rattled the fans. Hubbell just wasn't the type of pitcher to give free passes to opposing batsmen. In fact, the year before, Hubbell had walked only 47 men in 309 innings and in 1934, up to the July 10 All-Star Game, his control looked even better. (When the season was over, he had walked only 37 men in 313 innings.)

Worse yet, the National League's Hubbell had to face the American Leaguers' fearsome Murderer's Row—Babe Ruth, Lou Gehrig and Jimmie Foxx.

Though he was pitching before his own fans, Hubbell felt some hostility in the crowd.

"I could hear the guys in the stands yelling, 'Take him out before it's too late,' " Hubbell said.

His own National League teammates gathered around him after the walk to Manush. They wanted to be reassured.

"I'm all right," Hubbell told them.

Sure enough, the gangly lefthander was.

Babe Ruth was in the twilight of his career in 1934 but he still was a menacing slugger coming off a season in which he hit 34 homers and batted over .300. He still was a terror with men on base.

But Hubbell reared back, kicking his right foot high in the air, and let loose with his patented screwball. Hubbell threw three of them past Ruth, who looked as bewildered as he had ever been in his life. Three times the ball whizzed past Ruth, and three times the game's most famous slugger watched them go past without swinging. Ruth looked at the umpire as the third strike passed by him. He took the bat off his shoulder and headed back to the dugout. "He wasn't mad," Hubbell recalled later. "He just didn't believe it."

Hubbell may have been back in the groove but he had to face Gehrig next—and unlike Ruth he was at the peak of his career. He was in the midst of a season in which he would win the triple crown for leading the league in batting, home runs, and RBI's.

Hubbell coolly kept feeding screwballs past the other member of the Yankees' tandem. Gehrig was almost as befuddled as Ruth had been, and that was rare, for Gehrig was at his best with men on base. Hubbell needed four pitches to set down Gehrig for the second straight strikeout.

Jimmie Foxx was as fearsome as Gehrig. He had won the triple crown the year before with 48 homers, 163 RBI's and a .356 batting average. The star of the Philadelphia A's stared at his National League opponent as the two base runners got ready to move.

As Hubbell tossed a strike past Foxx, the base runners Gehringer and Manush worked a double steal. That meant that just one of Foxx' long singles could bring them home. Hubbell braced himself and threw another strike past Foxx. Then without a trace of fear, Hubbell got him on the third pitch.

King Carl had thrown ten pitches to three of the greatest sluggers ever—and struck all three of them out. He had defied all baseball odds.

But Hubbell wasn't through.

In the second inning, the American League's leadoff man was Al Simmons, a steady .300 hitter. The Chicago White Sox outfielder had reached .300 ten years in a row and was about to do it again in

1934. In 1930 and 1931 he had batted .381 and .390 to lead his league. Unawed, Hubbell struck him out, too. Then he struck out Joe Cronin, the Washington Senator shortstop who had batted over .300 for four straight years.

Never had one pitcher set down five dangerous future Hall of Famers in such fashion.

The spell couldn't last forever. Bill Dickey, the New York Yankees' ace catcher, singled to break it. But Hubbell came back strong to fan the pitcher, Lefty Gomez, for his sixth strikeout in two innings of All-Star play. He pitched one more inning of scoreless ball, then left the game with the National League in command, 4-0.

Without him, the National League All-Stars fell apart and lost, 9-7. But few were concerned with the final score when the Polo Grounds were emptied. Most of them agreed with league president Joe Heydler. He said it was the greatest feat he had seen in 60 years of watching baseball.

Now—and Forever—Pitching . . .

In his first time at bat as a major leaguer, Hoyt Wilhelm reared back and hit a home run. Only about three dozen men have ever done that in their first time up in the majors, and what's more, Wilhelm was an aspiring pitcher. But the most incredible aspect of that 1952 game, in retrospect, was that Wilhelm never hit another homer even though he played in more than 1,000 major-league games.

However, Hoyt Wilhelm stopped more than his share of potential home-run hitters in his record 1,070 appearances as a pitcher. He won a record total of 123 games as a reliever during his career as a big-league pitcher and saved a record 227 more games. Though relief pitching is a precarious way of making a living, Wilhelm went from the bullpen to the mound for 21 years, which may have been the most amazing feat of all for the rubbery-armed righthander.

Wilhelm was the kind of steady player that

teams loved to pick up in the heat of a pennant race. He was good almost to the end that way. In 1971, the year before he retired, he was released by the Atlanta Braves and seemingly was through at age forty-eight. But he signed with the Spokane, Wash., team in the minor leagues after he got his unconditional release from Atlanta—and made it back to the majors in September when Spokane's parent team, the Los Angeles Dodgers, needed a reliable arm in their quest for a National League pennant.

Wilhelm pitched in nine games for the Dodgers and gave up only two earned runs in 18 innings. His famed knuckleball could still baffle wide-eyed hitters half his age.

Anybody who knows baseball knows that the knuckleball takes less out of a pitcher physically than any other pitch short of a lob. Wilhelm was the first person to credit the pitch with prolonging his career.

"I don't say it doesn't take anything out of you at all," he said in his final season in the majors, "but I've never had to rear back and try to throw the ball by the hitters."

But 21 years is long by any standards. As baseball expert Milton Richman once wrote about the amazing Wilhelm's career, "Even those mechanical pitching machines break down before 30 years."

Strangely enough, Hoyt Wilhelm spent a decade pitching in the minors before he ever got to the big time. He signed as a nineteen-year-old in 1942. When he finally got to the majors, with the New York Giants in 1952, he was an immediate sensation. The Giants pitched him in relief for a near-record 71 games and Wilhelm responded by winning 15, losing only 3 and leading the National League with an earned run average of 2.43. He was the league's Rookie of the Year.

Wilhelm continued to make about 50 relief appearances a year until 1958, when the Cleveland Indians decided to give him a few starts. The rival Baltimore Orioles liked what they saw in the thirty-five-year-old starter and got him from Cleveland. Throughout 1959, Wilhelm was a full-time starter—and a good one.

Hoyt started 27 games and completed 13 of them for the Orioles in 1959. He pitched three shutouts and led the American League with a 2.19 earned run average. His 15-11 record was quite impressive considering the weak hitting team he played for.

But relief pitchers were becoming almost as valuable as starters by the end of the 1950's, so Baltimore moved him into the bullpen where he again began making about 50 appearances per year. He was traded to the Chicago White Sox in 1963. They used him mostly in relief, too, though he did start three games for them. After '63, Hoyt was strictly a bullpen man, making the

300-foot hike to the mound game after game in clutch situations.

In 1964, he won 12 games and saved 27 others for one of his finest seasons. For five straight years, he held his ERA below 2.00.

The years kept being added to his pitching record.

"At first, I felt I could hang on for five years," he said. "When I made five, I felt I could last ten. After that, I saw no reason why I couldn't go 15, then 20. And here I am."

At one point, he found himself pitching his knuckler in spring training to a befuddled young catcher who was born *after* Hoyt reached the majors.

Paul Richards, the clever baseball man who had Wilhelm in Baltimore, picked him up again in Atlanta and suggested in 1970 that Hoyt could probably pitch "another hundred years."

But time eventually caught up with him in 1972, when he made his last big-league appearance with the Los Angeles Dodgers. As he attended his final spring training sessions, he was asked what was the biggest change he had seen in baseball during more than two decades.

Wilhelm's answer was fitting: "I'd have to say it's got to do with the relief pitcher. He's become more predominant."

Relief Is Just a Second Away

Anyone who has heard all those television commercials about how you can get relief in minutes can appreciate the feats of some minor-league relief pitchers who provided relief in seconds.

Take Tony Komisar, a former lefthander for the Leesburg Braves in the Florida State League. He came into the nightcap of a 1956 game with Daytona Beach and faced a tough ninth-inning assignment. His team was ahead, 6-3, but Daytona Beach had the bases loaded. On his first pitch, the batter lined to the third baseman, who quickly tagged the base for the second out and relayed the ball to second for a triple play. One pitch, three outs. For Komisar, it was sweet revenge. Earlier in the day, he lost a 12-inning pitching duel to the same Daytona Beach team.

Bill Harrington, pitching relief for Charleston, W. Va., of the American Association, matched Komisar's three-kills-on-one pitch a year later in a game against Louisville. Harrington got a little relief himself out of the accomplishment, because he was protecting a three-run lead with the bases loaded when a Louisville slugger hit what seemed to be a sure home run smash to centerfield. As the baserunners began to head for home, Harrington's centerfielder made a miraculous catch and threw the ball into second base for the second out and then it was sent on to third for the triple play.

Bruce Haroldson also got three out on one pitch when he was hurling for Lewistown, Idaho, in the 1950s.

Steve Kraly of the Nashville team in the Southern Association didn't get three outs on one pitch, but he once collected two victories by facing just two men. It happened in 1959 when the lefthander was pitching relief. On June 9, he came into a game against Mobile with his team behind in the ninth inning. There were two outs. Kraly struck out the only man he faced, then sat back and watched Nashville rally for three runs in the bottom of the inning to win for him, 4-3.

Three days later, Kraly made his next appearance. This time he came in with two outs in the eighth and his team again on the short end of the score. Kraly got the opposing Atlanta player to ground out. Then he was lifted for a pinch hitter, who conveniently helped Nashville rally and take a 3-2 victory. Kraly had won again.

Major leaguers also turn in some astounding relief feats. In 1956, Chicago Cub pitcher Jim Davis was trying to slow down the St. Louis Cardinals. The southpaw did it in the sixth when he struck out Hal Smith, Jim Brandt and Lindy McDaniel. But the last pitch to McDaniel got away from Davis' catcher, allowing a man on third to score and McDaniel to get to first safely. Davis wasn't rattled by his ill fate. He calmly struck out Don Blasingame—his fourth "K" of the inning—to become the first pitcher since 1916 to fan four in a single inning.

There's no record of a major leaguer getting three outs on a single pitch, but Ray Moore of the Kansas City Athletics deserves mention for his performance in relief against the Chicago White Sox in 1960.

Moore came into a wide-open 9-9 game with the bases loaded in the ninth and only one out. It wasn't a pleasant assignment. Moore got Chicago's Bill Tuttle to hit into a double play on his first pitch to retire the side. Then he watched little Nellie Fox slug a rare home run to win the game for him. One pitch, one victory.

NO-HITTERS

The Most Perfect Innings in Baseball History

In the visitors' clubhouse of Milwaukee's County Stadium, on May 26, 1959, pitcher Harvey Haddix ran down the Milwaukee Braves' lineup for the benefit of his teammates and methodically told how he planned to pitch to each opponent. It was routine stuff for the Pittsburgh Pirates' lefthanded hurler and his teammates. But this night, one of the Pirate players offered a comment to encourage Haddix, who had not been getting much onfield support.

"That was a good rundown, Harvey," said third baseman Don Hoak. "You go out there and pitch to those guys exactly like that and you'll pitch a no-hitter."

As it turned out, Haddix did more than that.

The first man to face Haddix that evening was the Braves' Johnny O'Brien. Haddix tested his fastball on O'Brien and came up with a strike. Next he tried his slider and that too was on target. He made a quick decision to rely on those pitches for the rest of the night.

Haddix, a thirty-three-year-old hurler with a sketchy big-league career, got O'Brien and the rest of the side out in the first, and again in the second. Pirate shortstop Dick Schofield made a leaping snare of a line drive that looked headed for a safety in the third. That play and Schofield's long-throw out of a deep ground ball in the sixth inning were two of the few challenges Haddix would get. Otherwise, he was getting out every Brave who faced him in the order they faced him.

It occurred to Haddix that he had a no-hitter going because the scoreboard faced him, and the crowd, even though it was pro-Milwaukee, was rallying behind him. But it didn't dawn on Haddix that he was pitching a perfect game.

Besides, Haddix had other problems to worry about. He personally was off to a good start that season, but his teammates just weren't giving him much scoring support. The Pirates were repeating their lackluster offense this night, too, even though they were getting more than their share of hits off the Braves' Lou Burdette.

In fact, the Pirates were to get 12 hits for the game. But all of them were singles. In the third inning alone, the Pirates got three hits and did not score; one of the singles hitters had been thrown on when he tried to stretch an extra base out of a teammate's single.

With two outs in the ninth, Haddix had a perfect game at the brink—something only four other pitchers had done in the majors in the twentieth century. When Burdette, the 27th batter, came up to the plate, he shouted out something about breaking up the no-hitter. Haddix may have been rattled somewhat by the opposing pitcher's comment, because he brought the count to 2-2. Then his catcher, Smokey Burgess, called for a slider to polish off Burdette. Haddix sent a good one that Burdette swung at and missed. It was his eighth strikeout.

Haddix had his perfect nine innings—but no victory yet.

Still, the Milwaukee crowd of 19,000 stood up and gave him a rousing cheer.

The Pirates came to bat in the top of the tenth eager to help their masterful pitcher claim his piece of history. With one out and a man on first base, hefty Dick Stuart, the team's home-run hitter, smacked a ball that carried all the way to the centerfield fence. But the Braves' Andy Pafko chased it down and prevented the run.

Since the scoreboard at County Stadium registered only ten innings, Haddix lost track of just how well he was doing. He became confused as to what inning it was.

But he continued to check the Braves in perfect fashion, getting them out in order in the tenth, eleventh and twelfth innings, too. No pitcher before or since has ever pitched more than the full nine innings of perfect ball. Haddix had seen 36 men come up and he sent them all back frustrated.

The 165-pounder saw his team go stale in the thirteenth inning, too. He also saw them tensing up a bit in the field. In the bottom of the thirteenth inning, Haddix' string of perfection came to an end. Don Hoak's throwing error after a grounder by Felix Mantilla let the Braves' leadoff man get on first. The Pirates made a feeble protest that Mantilla had made a wrong turn at first, but the complaint was not allowed.

Mantilla was sacrificed to second base, so strategy dictated that Haddix should intentionally walk the next batter, Hank Aaron, which he did. It was the only walk Haddix would give up all night.

Joe Adcock, the Braves' husky first baseman, was the next man up. He had struck out twice and grounded out two other times to become a routine victim for Haddix. But in the thirteenth, Haddix slipped a pitch at him that was just too high. Haddix realized that fact when he let the ball go. By then, it was too late. Adcock got under the pitch and lifted it toward left-center. The Pirates' Bill Virdon, who had made two fine deep catches in the tenth inning, raced furiously and leaped for the ball—but it was slightly over the fence and out of reach. Mantilla jaunted toward home to score.

Yet in a strange wrapup to a strange game, Aaron left the playing field after touching second base. Braves players and fans yelled for him to continue circling the bases but Aaron didn't hear them until it was too late; Adcock had already passed him. Due to the technicality, which wasn't resolved till the next day, Haddix lost 1-0 instead of 3-0. It was hardly much consolation for the man who had pitched the most consecutive perfect innings in baseball history.

Haddix's 12 Perfect Innings

Pittsburgh	AB	R	H	P	A	E
Schofield, ss	6	0	3	2	4	0
Virdon, cf	6	0	1	8	0	0
Burgess, c	5	0	0	8	0	0
Nelson, 1b	5	0	2	14	0	0
Skinner, lf	5	0	1	4	0	0
Mazeroski, 2b	5	0	1	1	1	0
Hoak, 3b	5	0	2	0	6	1
Mejias, rf	3	0	1	1	0	0
aStuart	1	0	0	0	0	0
Christopher, rf	1	0	0	0	0	0
Haddix, p	5	0	1	0	2	0
Totals	47	0	12	c38	13	1

Milwaukee	AB	R	H	P	A	E
O'Brien, 2b	3	0	0	2	5	0
bRice	1	0	0	0	0	0
Mantilla, 2b	1	1	0	1	2	0
Mathews, 3b	4	0	0	2	3	0
Aaron, rf	4	0	0	1	0	0
Adcock, 1b	5	0	1	17	3	0
Covington, lf	4	0	0	4	0	0
Crandall, c	4	0	0	2	1	0
Pafko, cf	4	0	0	6	0	0
Logan, ss	4	0	0	3	5	0
Burdette, p	4	0	0	1	3	0
Totals	38	1	1	39	22	0

```
Pittsburgh .........  0 0 0  0 0 0  0 0 0  0 0 0   0—0
Milwaukee .........  0 0 0  0 0 0  0 0 0  0 0 0   1—1
```

aFlied out for Mejias in tenth. bFlied out for O'Brien in tenth. cTwo out when game ended. Run batted in—Adcock. Two-base hit—Adcock. Sacrifice hit—Mathews. Double plays— Adcock, Logan and Adcock; Mathews, O'Brien and Adcock; Adcock and Logan. Left on bases—Pittsburgh 8, Milwaukee 1. Bases on balls—Off Haddix 1 (Aaron). Struck out—By Haddix 8 (Adcock 2, Burdette 3, O'Brien, Mathews, Pafko), by Burdette 2 (Mazeroski, Hoak). Runs and earned runs—Haddix 1-0. Burdette 0-0. Winning pitcher—Burdette (8-2). Losing pitcher—Haddix (3-3). Umpires—Smith, Dascoli, Secory and Dixon. Time of game—2:54. Attendance—19,194.

The Losing Pitcher Who Was a Big Winner

The Detroit Tigers had gone 52 years without ever finishing in last place in their league—an amazing stretch that no other team could claim in 1952. But that year their luck ran out and they floundered miserably from start to finish, 45 games behind the league-leading New York Yankees. Good players turned sour over night. Those who played well got little support from their teammates, so their talents were unnoticed.

One such victim was Virgil (Fire) Trucks, the thirty-three-year-old fastball pitcher who once set an organized baseball record for strikeouts with 418 for a minor-league team. Trucks, when going right, was a potential 20-game winner. He had reached 19 one season and in ten major-league campaigns had never had a losing season.

But in 1952, the roof caved in on him, too.

That year, Trucks pitched in 35 games. He started 29. He won only five, compared to 19 losses.

If there was ever a better pitcher when he was

winning, however, it would have been a miracle. That season, Trucks' five victories included two no-hitters, a one-hitter, a two-hitter and a six-hitter. Considering that the Tigers had not had a no-hit performance in some 40 years, Trucks' achievements are all the more amazing.

Trucks' first no-hitter in the majors (he had had four in the minors) came against the Washington Senators on May 15, 1952. The burly pitcher didn't pitch that impressively, however, as no-hitters go. He hit two batters, walked another and saw one man get on by error. It took a ninth-inning home run by Vic Wertz to give him a 1-0 victory.

Victories came few and far between after that. In another encounter with the Senators, Trucks no-hit them after giving up a single in the first inning. By the time the Tigers departed for an Eastern swing in August, Trucks was on the trading block, and players were coming and going by the numbers in Detroit. The team was playing so poorly that not one sportswriter among Detroit's three major daily newspapers bothered to accompany the team to New York for an August 25 game with the Yankees. Trucks, with a mere 4-15 record, was about to take on the best team in baseball.

Trucks' control was remarkably better than it had been for most of the year, including the first no-hitter, as he began leveling the Yankees. He was loose and mixing his pitches and relying on control more than on his vaunted fastball.

He set down the Yankees in the first and second innings, then ran into a small problem in the third. It was then that Phil Rizzuto slapped a grounder at Tiger shortstop Johnny Pesky, who seemed to have trouble getting the ball out of his glove. When Pesky did free up the ball, he made a late and low throw to first base. Rizzuto got on.

The official scorer first gave Pesky an error. Then, after checking with press box colleagues, he changed it to a hit. The scoreboard listed a hit and that's the way it stayed until the seventh inning. Then, during the stretch, an announcement was made that the decision had been reversed back to an error after further consultation.

The crowd of 13,442 Yankee fans suddenly came alive. Some of them may have seen Allie Reynolds pitch two no-hitters the year before, but that was for a championship team. The Tigers were nobodies.

As the game wore on, Trucks got better and better. After allowing three men on in the first inning (one by a walk, two by errors), Trucks bore down and retired batter after batter. In the meantime, Steve Souchak—Wertz' replacement—knocked in a run to give Trucks a 1-0 lead.

The Yankees had never been no-hitted before during a pennant race. But Trucks had their num-

45

ber that day. He continued his dominance until the final inning, then relied on a fastball to get him through his second no-hitter of the year. As it was, he retired the final 22 Yankees in a row. Again he won, 1-0, for his final moment of success in a rather unusual year.

The following season Trucks was traded not once but twice. Strangely enough, 1953 turned out to be his first 20-game winning year.

The Only World Series No-Hitter

Perfect was not the best word to use in describing pitcher Don Larsen. "Fun-loving," "carousing," and "Peck's Bad Boy" were used more often. The big 6-foot, 4-inch strongman with the face of a movie star had a casual aura about him, even in what hardened baseball people considered the most crucial situations. The New York *Times* once reported that, "On a Yankee squad that includes a liberal share of *bon vivants*, Larsen has had the reputation of being one of the gayest blades."

Larsen seemed to have his own set of training rules. That got him in trouble more than once. As for not making the best of his talents, the Yankees returned him to the minors in 1955, his first year with the club, as sort of a shape-up side-trip.

But Larsen had talent to spare. The Yankees got him in the first place—as one of the key figures in an 18-man trade—despite the fact that he was a miserable 3-21 with the Baltimore Orioles in 1954. That first season with the Yankees, Larsen was recalled in late July from his minor-league demotion, and posted an 8-1 record to help the team win the American League pennant. He celebrated the strong finish the next spring by driving his brand new convertible into a telephone pole at 5 A.M. after a late date.

The Yankees kept him throughout 1956, however, because he was resourceful on the pitching mound, at least. He posted an 11-5 record as a part-time starter and long reliever.

"The big feller can be one of the greatest if he wants to be," Casey Stengel, the Yankee manager, used to say often about the 220-pound Larsen. Stengel used to marvel at all Larsen's talents—his ability to hit and field and run the bases as well as pitch. Larsen was sometimes used as a pinch hitter and pinch runner, too.

But in general the "big feller" didn't have a distinguished major-league career. He stuck around for 14 years but won only 81 games and lost 91.

For one day, though, Larsen was as perfect as any pitcher can be. It happened on October 8, 1956, during his second year with the Yankees.

There was nothing unusual about the day except for the fact that Stengel decided to take a chance with Larsen in the fifth World Series game against the powerful Brooklyn Dodgers. It was a chancy move for several reasons, the main one being Larsen's sometimes erratic moves. Stengel had seen Larsen get rattled in the second game of the 1956 Series, when he went into the second inning with a 6-0 lead and began to blow it. Larsen was yanked and the Dodgers went on to win the game, 13-8. But Casey was having trouble with his pitchers and went to Larsen in the fifth game, with the Series tied, three days after the 13-8 débacle.

Larsen had one strong point: He didn't let games affect him beforehand. The twenty-seven-year-old righthander prepped for his third World Series start (he had been shelled in a game the year before, too) by having a few beers and turning in past midnight. "I just did like I always do," he said nonchalantly.

But the next day, before a packed crowd of 64,000 at Yankee Stadium, he did more than usual.

Larsen got hooked up in a pitching duel with the Dodgers' toughened Sal Maglie. Larsen set down the first 12 Dodgers to face him. Not one of them got to base. Maglie meanwhile mowed down the first 11 Yankees he encountered.

A home run by the Yankees' Mickey Mantle broke the ice in the bottom of the fourth. But Larsen's spell over the Dodgers continued.

Larsen was getting some help. Yogi Berra behind the plate was handling Larsen beautifully, mixing up his array of fastballs, sliders and slow curves. Afield, the Yanks were contributing their usual collection of outstanding plays, too. Gil McDougald snatched a hard-hit ball by Jackie Robinson off the ground after it had caromed from third baseman Andy Carey's glove; McDougald made the throw to first to get Robinson. Mantle made a brilliant dash to get a long-hit ball by Gil Hodges in the fifth inning.

But the triumph was mostly Larsen's as he handled a lineup including a half dozen Hall of Fame prospects with relative ease. Only once did Larsen give as many as three balls to one batter. Seven times he struck out Dodger batters. Only four balls could even be considered potent hits under the right conditions, and one of those four was a foul.

The Yankees got an insurance run when Hank Bauer homered. Then they nervously watched Larsen try to pitch the first perfect game since 1922. The idea of attempting the feat in the World Series added to the tension. In fact, no pitcher had ever hurled a no-hitter in World Series play.

Larsen continued to dazzle the likes of Roy Campanella, Pee Wee Reese, Duke Snider, Carl Furillo, Robinson and Hodges with his no-windup delivery. And with the game less than two hours old, it came down to Larsen versus pinch hitter Dale Mitchell, an ex-American Leaguer with a .312 lifetime batting average. Mitchell was filling in for Maglie.

There were two outs in the ninth and Larsen had retired 26 men in a row.

Larsen first threw a ball. The stadium was so quiet you could almost hear the sweat roll down the players' faces. Larsen got back on target; he next threw to a corner and came up with a called strike. Mitchell swung at the next pitch and missed. Then he fouled a ball. Mitchell had been taking his time, which rattled Larsen a little bit. But the pitcher countered this strategy by throwing fast—and hard.

His next pitch was a fastball that zoomed over the plate. Umpire Babe Pinelli promptly called it strike three—the clincher to what may have been baseball's best-pitched game considering the circumstances and the competition.

Despite the jubilation, Larsen's celebration included a court order from his wife, whom he had left, trying to tie up his World Series share.

The Fifth Game

Brooklyn Dodgers	AB	R	H	P	A	E
Gilliam, 2b	3	0	0	2	0	0
Reese, ss	3	0	0	4	2	0
Snider, cf	3	0	0	1	0	0
Robinson, 3b	3	0	0	2	4	0
Hodges, 1b	3	0	0	5	1	0
Amoros, lf	3	0	0	3	0	0
Furillo, rf	3	0	0	0	0	0
Campanella, c	3	0	0	7	2	0
Maglie, p	2	0	0	0	1	0
a-Mitchell	1	0	0	0	0	0
Totals	27	0	0	24	10	0

New York Yankees	AB	R	H	P	A	E
Bauer, rf	4	0	1	4	0	0
Collins, 1b	4	0	1	7	0	0
Mantle, cf	3	1	1	4	0	0
Berra, c	3	0	0	7	0	0
Slaughter, lf	2	0	0	1	0	0
Martin, 2b	3	0	1	3	4	0
McDougald, ss	2	0	0	0	2	0
Carey, 3b	3	1	1	1	1	0
Larsen, p	2	0	0	0	1	0
Totals	26	2	5	27	8	0

Brooklyn	0	0 0	0 0 0	0 0	0—0
New York	0	0 0	1 0 1	0 0	*—2

a—Called out on strikes for Maglie in ninth. Errors—None. Runs batted in—Mantle, Bauer. Home run—Mantle. Sacrifice—Larsen. Double plays—Reese and Hodges; Hodges, Campanella, Robinson, Campanella and Robinson. Left on bases—Brooklyn 0, New York 3. Bases on balls—Off Maglie 2 (Slaughter, McDougald). Struck out—By Larsen 7 (Gilliam, Reese, Hodges, Campanella, Snider, Maglie, Mitchell); Maglie 5 (Martin, Collins 2, Larsen, Bauer). Runs and earned runs—Off Maglie 2 and 2. Winning pitcher—Larsen. Losing pitcher—Maglie. Umpires—Pinelli (N.), plate; Soar (A.), first base; Boggess (N.), second base; Napp (A.), third base; Gorman (N.), left field; and Runge (A.), right field. Time of game—2:06. Attendance—64,519 (paid).

The High School Kid With An 0.18 ERA

The Texas Rangers had heard so much about a high-school phenom in 1973 that they decided to send their key front-office personnel out to watch eighteen-year-old David Clyde pitch. Rangers owner Bob Short, general manager Joe Burke, manager Whitey Herzog and pitching coach Chuck Estrada all ventured out to a high-school field in Dallas when Clyde came to town with his Houston Westchester High team.

Clyde didn't disappoint them. He went about his business of pitching his ninth no-hitter of the year against Dallas' Kimball High, striking out two batters every inning and getting a 1-0 victory.

If Clyde wasn't the most sensational high-school pitcher ever, he had to be close. He completed his senior year with an 18-0 record. His earned run average was a next-to-nothing 0.18. Clyde struck out 328 batters in 148 innings.

His no-hitter in front of the Rangers' management paid off handsomely for the lefthander, too. When the baseball draft of free agents was held that year, the Rangers made him the first player to be taken. They paid him a $125,000 bonus to assure that they would get him, too.

Nineteen days after he graduated from high school, he was on the mound for the Rangers, pitching a 4-3 victory.

In no time at all, the Rangers got that bonus money back. Clyde drew over 113,000 fans for his first four starts.

LONG BALL
SLUGGERS

The Tape-Measure Homers

Mickey Mantle was a country boy who could hit the ball a country mile. Mantle was a mere twenty-one years old when the crusty New York Yankee Manager Casey Stengel made the comment, "He is probably the most powerful switch hitter the game has ever known." Stengel was perhaps a little partial to his own player, but his baseball wisdom had been accumulated over four decades at the time. Besides, the year he made the comment—1953—Casey had some other figures to back him up.

Mantle was a third-year major leaguer at the time and just coming into his own as a home-run hitter. He had hit 37 doubles in 1952, but at twenty-one he was better muscled and getting his full 175 pounds into the swing.

In 1953 his home runs weren't just dropping over fences—they were going well beyond them. It was Mantle who created a new, though unofficial, statistic called the "tape-measure homer." He turned sportswriters and public relations men into surveyors when he awed them with his long-distance booms.

Mantle gave a preview of things to come for the 1953 season in an exhibition game at Pittsburgh's Forbes Field on the eve of the regular season. Batting lefthanded, he poled a ball over the rightfield seats and out of the ballpark, a feat only two men (one was Babe Ruth) had ever done.

Then eight days later, on April 17, Mantle struck again.

Lefthander Chuck Stobbs was one of the better pitchers on the old Washington Senators team, so Mantle naturally batted righthanded against him. The regular season was under way at the time.

Mantle got hold of one of Stobbs' pitches and launched it toward the bleachers in left-center. The ball picked up momentum plus a bit of a tailwind as it sailed over the heads of the fans at Griffith Stadium. It passed the 460-foot mark, where they sat, then bounced off a 60-foot-high sign. It came to a rest in a backyard. The figure filberts were so intrigued they measured the distance. It turned out to be 565 feet from home plate.

Other balls, perhaps off the bat of Babe Ruth, may have gone further. Ruth supposedly blasted one over 600 feet in an exhibition game in St. Petersburg, Fla. But Mantle's blow was measured and to this day is the standard for long-distance hitters.

Mantle grew to be 195 pounds and a more powerful hitter than he was in 1953. Three years later he came close to poking a ball out of Yankee Stadium; it hit the façade at the top of the third deck in rightfield. The opposing pitcher was Pedro Ramos of Washington. In 1963, he tagged a ball pitched by the Kansas City Athletics' reliever Bill Fischer and sent it to nearly the same place. It was still rising when it crashed off a 108-foot-high façade atop the third deck. Statisticians estimated the ball would have traveled perhaps 620 feet without the obstruction. A year later, he got his power behind a pitch by Ray Herbert of the Chicago White Sox and sent it over 500 feet into dead centerfield at Yankee Stadium for the longest measured homer at that historic park.

But none of the Herculean homers matched the 565-footer back in 1953, when Mantle was just getting started in the tape-measure business.

The "730-Foot" Homer

Gil Carter was an all-around athlete and a "slugger" in every sport he took up. As a 210-pound heavyweight, he won 61 of 68 bouts. As a football player, he made all-state in Kansas for his hard-hitting plunges from fullback. But it was in baseball that he really made a name for himself with his hard hitting.

Playing for Carlsbad, N. M., of the Sophomore League in 1959, the twenty-three-year-old outfielder was zooming in on that minor league's home-run record. He finally got the record with his 28th of the season on August 11—and left a few people gaping in disbelief in the process.

Homer No. 28 for Carter took off like a shot toward the leftfield fence. It was still rising when it soared over a light tower 360 feet from home plate. The ball kept on going, crossing a street, two alleys and two lots. Then it disappeared from sight. Later, a developer of a subdivision behind the ballpark found the ball beside a house, 730 feet from home plate. En route to the house it knocked some peaches from a tree.

The people who took the time to analyze the homer said it had to travel at least 650 feet before the bounces and rolls that carried it to the 730-foot mark. Nobody has officially recorded the longest home run in history, but the hard-hitting Carter has to be right up there with the distance sluggers.

The 70-Foot "Homer"

What may have been the shortest home run on record in major-league baseball occurred one hot summer day in 1914 at Washington Park in Brooklyn. It happened in a Federal League game between the Brooklyn Feds and the Chicago Whales. The league was considered an "outlaw circuit" by the American and National Leagues but nevertheless it was made up of very good teams and players, and has been accorded major-league status by most baseball historians.

Only two umpires handled a game in those

days—one behind the plate and another in the infield. But one of the umpires failed to show for a regularly scheduled game at Washington Park on a very hot summer day. The other ump, Bill Brennan, decided to work the game by himself.

Brennan got tired of running to the home dugout for new balls each time he ran out, so before the fifth inning he built a pyramid of them behind the pitcher's mound, from where he was calling balls and strikes.

In the fifth, Brooklyn catcher Grover Land, who had only three homers to show for his five years with the Cleveland Indians in the American League, smacked a line drive into the pile of balls about 70 feet away and splattered them in all directions. Land took off running for first, realizing that he had created a rare confusion.

The Chicago infielders couldn't sort through the balls to find out which was the right one, so they conveniently picked up any ball near them and tagged away at Land as he circled the bases. Land just kept on running. When he reached home plate, the Chicago catcher was waiting for him with one of the balls, too—but the overworked umpire disregarded that tag also.

Land was given credit for an "inside the park" homer.

72 *Home Runs One Season*

Babe Ruth's major-league home-run record of 60 in one season seemed out of sight during the early years of the 1950's. But for a gigantic minor leaguer who would never make the majors, the Ruthian-size records were not so significant. In four years, from 1952 through 1955, Joltin' Joe Bauman slugged 221 home runs—an average of more than 58 a season.

Bauman, a strapping 6-foot, 5-inch, 240-pound first baseman, had been counted out of the major-league picture by scouts when he began his spree in 1952. He was already thirty years old, and he pretty much muffed his big-league hopes when he clubbed only 11 home runs and batted .275 for the Hartford, Conn., team of the Eastern League back in 1948. The Eastern League was Class A in those days, and that's as high as Bauman ever got as a Boston Brave farmhand. The fact that the Braves were a pennant winner in 1948 left them with little time to groom Bauman for the majors even though he had smashed 48 and 38 homers in two previous seasons. Bauman himself studied the situation and figured it hopeless, dropping out of organized ball to play for a semi-pro team in Oklahoma after the 1948 season.

But pro ball lured Bauman back in 1952. He got reinstated and joined the Artesia, N. M., team of the Class C Longhorn League.

It took little time for Joe Bauman to get back in the groove. He smacked an even 50 homers that season and had the league's pitchers so shaken up that on one occasion a righthanded hurler actually pitched lefthanded to the lefthanded-hitting Bauman in an effort to stymie him. (The strategy worked, by the way. In one of the few—if not the only—cases of ambidextrous pitching on record, Audie Malone of the Roswell team carried Bauman to a 3-2 count and then struck him out with a slow curve!)

Mostly, Bauman tore up the league and became a local hero. He hit 53 more home runs for Artesia in 1953, then joined the Roswell team in another New Mexico city. Come 1954 and the slugging first baseman, who had been playing minor-league baseball since 1941, began making history. He had his eye set on the all-time organized baseball record of 69 homers, established by Joe Hauser of the Minneapolis team of the American Association back in 1933, and tied by Bob Crues of the Amarillo, Texas, team in 1948.

The former Oklahoman zeroed in on that mark on August 31 when he smashed four homers against Sweetwater to bring his total up to 68. That left Bauman four games in which to match or surpass Hauser, an ex-Philadelphia Athletic who had made his mark after a six-year major-league stay, and Crues.

In his next game, Bauman just missed the fence by inches as he lined a long-shot foul. Then on September 2, he caught Hauser with his 69th.

Bauman had accomplished his first 69 in only 136 games, which was remarkable in its own right. Hauser, for example, needed 154 games for his feat and Crues 140.

Now Bauman had two more games—a September 5 doubleheader at his old stomping grounds in Artesia—in which he could claim the record for himself. The twinbill evoked enough interest to draw an overflow 2,600 fans to NuMex Park.

Bauman tried not to let them down. In the first inning, after taking a 2-2 count from the pitcher, Bauman fouled off two more pitches. Then boom! The Roswell Rocket lofted the ball 360 feet and over the fence for home run No. 70. He could now relax.

Bauman's idea of relaxing was to smack home runs. He got two more in the second game to bring his season total to 72 in just 136 games. No one has threatened that record very seriously since 1954.

Naturally Bauman had his share of critics—the people who scoffed at the Class C level of play, the depleted minor-league ranks because of the Korean War, and the short fences that minor leaguers enjoy. But an overall look at Bauman's 1954 season lends luster to his accomplishments.

In addition to his 72 home runs in 498 official at-bats, Joe batted an even .400 and drove in 224 runs for a second-place team. He struck out 99 times while he was swinging for the big ones, but he also was hampered in his quest by 150 walks.

His homers were a fraction over half of the team's total of 143.

As for the short fences, well. . . .

After the windup of the regular season, Roswell entered the Longhorn League playoffs. In one game, against Carlsbad, Joe Bauman tagged a ball and sent it flying approximately 500 feet. Few big leaguers have hit one that far.

The 60-Home-Run Club
(In Organized Baseball)

HR	Player	Team	League	Class	Year	Batted
72	Joe Bauman	Roswell, N. Mex.	Longhorn	C	1954	L
69	Joe Hauser	Minneapolis	Amer. Assn.	AA	1933	L
69	Bob Crues	Amarillo	W. Tex.-N. Mex.	C	1948	R
66	Dick Stuart	Lincoln, Nebr.	Western	A	1956	R
64	Bob Lennon	Nashville	Southern	AA	1954	L
63	Joe Hauser	Baltimore	International	AA	1930	L
62	John Clabaugh	Tyler	East Texas	D	1926	L
62	Ken Guettler	Shreveport, La.	Texas	AA	1956	R
61	Roger Maris	N.Y. Yankees	American	Majors	1961	L
60	Tony Lazzeri	Salt Lake City	Pacific Coast	AA	1925	R
60	Babe Ruth	N.Y. Yankees	American	Majors	1927	L
60	Forest Kennedy	Plainview, Tex.	Southwestern	B	1956	R

Long Balls and Short Fences

The Corsicana team of the Texas League was loaded with good hitters in 1902, so many in fact that a promising young Canadian-born prospect named Justin (Nig) Clarke was placed seventh in the batting order. Clarke, a nineteen-year-old catcher destined for the major leagues, could not complain, however. Corsicana was so good that it busted the Texas League pennant race wide open by winning 27 straight games. It was one of the best minor-league clubs ever assembled.

But after a June 15 game with Texarkana, the "Oil City" team may have wondered if they had underestimated the teenage backstop. That day he had eight official at-bats and eight shots at the short (estimated at 200 to 220 feet) fence of the ballpark at Ennis, Texas. He made the best of them—by slugging eight home runs.

All in all, Clarke had 32 total bases and batted in 16 runs. The box score for the day shows him with a stolen base, which indicates he may have gotten on base by a walk, too.

Clarke carried the brunt of the attack that Sunday afternoon. But he wasn't the only hero for Corsicana. The box score shows the Oil City's Bill Alexander, the shortstop, and Ike Pendleton, the leftfielder and cleanup man, with 8-for-8 at the plate, too. Alexander and first baseman Mike O'Connor each smacked three homers, and the rest of the Corsicana team combined for seven more. The 21 home runs were instrumental in Corsicana's 51-3 victory.

For years, Clarke's feat came under close scrutiny because one box score of the day had him listed as scoring only three runs. But the team's shortstop and also the club owner made sworn affidavits that Clarke indeed smacked eight homers.

Perhaps the skepticism arose over the fact that Clarke, as a nine-year veteran in the majors, had a grand total of six big-league home runs.

But for the day in 1902, he was supreme.

Below is the box score for the game. Obviously a few totals don't jive and a 2-hour 10-minute contest seems suspect for a game in which more than 100 players went to bat (for both teams). But in a 51-3 game, even the scorekeeper shouldn't be expected to turn in an errorless performance.

Incredible Baseball Feats

The Box Score

Corsicana	AB	R	H	P	A	E
Maloney cf	6	5	3	5	0	0
Alexander, 2b	8	5	8	4	5	0
Ripley, rf	8	6	5	0	0	0
Pendleton, lf	8	6	8	1	2	0
Markley, 3b	7	7	6	3	4	0
O'Connor, 1b	8	7	7	8	0	0
Clarke, c	8	8	8	3	1	0
Morris, ss	8	6	6	3	4	0
Wright, p	4	1	2	0	2	0
Totals	65	51	53	27	18	0

Texarkana	AB	R	H	P	A	E
Deskin, cf	5	1	2	6	1	0
Mulkey, 2b	4	0	1	0	2	1
Welter, 3b	4	0	1	2	2	2
Wolfe, c	4	1	1	2	2	0
Murphy, lf	4	0	1	3	1	0
DeWitt, p	3	0	1	0	2	0
Tackaberry, 1b	4	1	1	9	0	0
Gillon rf	4	0	1	1	0	0
Burns, ss	4	0	0	4	3	2
Totals	36	3	9	27	13	5

Texarkana .... 0 1 0 0 0 0 0 2 0— 3
Corsicana .... 6 2 9 2 7 5 4 8 8—51

Stolen bases—Maloney, Alexander, Morris, Clarke, Ripley. Three-base hits—Markley, O'Connor. Home Runs—Maloney, Alexander 3, Ripley 2, Pendleton 2, Markley, O'Connor 3, Clarke 8, Morris. Two-base hits—Morris, Alexander, Maloney, Pendleton, Deskin, Tackaberry, Welter. Double plays—Morris to Alexander to O'Connor, Morris to Alexander, Alexander to Morris to O'Connor, Markley to Alexander to O'Connor, Burns to Tackaberry. Left on bases—Corsicana 15, Texarkana 5. Bases on balls—off Wright 1, DeWitt 3. Struck out by Wright 2, DeWitt 1. Hit by pitcher—by DeWitt 3. Earned runs—Corsicana 26, Texarcana 1. Umpires—Method and Cavender (players). Time 2:10.

70

Minor-league baseball has a fascinating history of strange happenings when big men take big bats and go after little outfield walls.

Here are some of the forgotten home-run performances throughout the years.

1914: On June 5, pitcher John Cantley of the Opelika, Ala., team of the Georgia-Alabama League slammed three home runs with the bases loaded, batted in a total of 19 runs, and hurled his club to a 19-1 victory over Talladega, Ala.

1922: On August 13, Hastings and Lincoln of the Nebraska League staged a slugfest in which 20 home runs were hit in a doubleheader. The teams made 53 hits and 45 runs in all. The result: they split the twinbill.

1923: On May 11, Pete Schneider, playing for the Vernon team of the Pacific Coast League, had five homers—two of which came with the bases loaded—versus Salt Lake City.

1930: On August 6, Gene Rye of the Waco team in the Texas League smacked three home runs against Beaumont—in the *same* inning.

1947: In seven playoff games, Bill Serena slugged 13 home runs for the Lubbock, Texas, team of the West Texas-New Mexico League. Though the 13 home runs didn't count in his regular-season total, they unofficially gave him 70 for the year.

1948: In August, Bob Crues of the Amarillo, Texas, team of the West Texas-New Mexico League blasted out 20 homers in a month. He finished the year with 69. Also that year, Al Rosen of Kansas City of the American Association twice had home-run sprees. In June he pounded out 5-for-5 in 17 innings during a doubleheader and in July he hit five more in a row during a two-game stretch.

1954: Ray Perry, the playing manager of the Bakersfield team in the California League, totaled 37 homers to lead his loop in that department at age thirty-four. It was the seventh straight year that Perry had won a home-run title in the minors, having led the Far West League from 1948 through 1951 and the Cotton States League in 1952-53.

1955: On August 2, John Romano, a catcher for the Waterloo, Iowa, team of the Three-I League hit another homer—the ninth night in a row he accomplished the feat. The twenty-year-old Romano missed a homer in one game of a doubleheader during the streak, but otherwise had at least one for each evening. The future big-league catcher saw his string stopped on August 3. That night, he drove a ball above the outfield fence— but a Peoria player made a leaping catch over the top of the outfield barrier to snare the well-hit ball. Romano finished the season with 38 homers.

1956: During a stretch on May 13-15, Al Weygandt of Topeka, Kan., of the Western League collected 10 home runs. On May 13, the twenty-five-year-old first baseman got two in the first game and three in the second during a twin bill against Amarillo. He got three more off Amarillo pitching the next day. Then on May 15, versus Albuquerque, he got two homers during the times at bat when he wasn't walked. When the Topeka team continued its road trip to Pueblo, Colo., a few days later, Weygandt continued his hot hitting, getting four more homers. That gave him 14 runs, seven other hits and 30 RBI's during 37 at-bats on the 10-game road trip.

1958: On August 19, a small crowd of just over 600 fans watched the Douglas Copper Kings of the Mexican League get one home run out of each starter in the lineup as they beat the Chihuahua Dorados, 22-8.

Finding the Fences in Many Ballparks

Back in the days before big-league baseball franchises became a floating crap game, bouncing from city to city as the season comes to an end, the great Babe Ruth set an impressive standard by hitting a homer in every American League ballpark for 11 straight years. Baseball was simple then; a league consisted of eight teams and they stayed put year after year.

A couple of other players made marathon marks, too, by hitting homers in all 15 possible parks—American and National Leagues—while they were playing. They were Harry Heilman and Johnny Mize. The latter reached his fifteenth different fence (two St. Louis teams shared the same park in those days) when he was 39 years old in 1952. In fact, Mize got his fifteenth ballpark in his portfolio by hitting a grand slammer in Washington that year.

Nowadays the old parks are replaced by new edifices and teams are shifted from television market area to television market area at the drop of a rating. When the lords of baseball run out of places to shift teams to, they expand the leagues. Baseball has gone from 16 teams in the era of Ruth, Heilman and Mize to 24—and they may not be done expanding yet.

The new alignments have made it simple to hit in more parks than 15, as Heilman and Mize had done.

But one of the premier players of recent times is making it difficult for his home-run slugging contemporaries to match him for "notches" on his bat.

Frank Robinson will someday make Baseball's Hall of Fame for many reasons, including his fourth-place listing on the all-time home-run hitting list (with nearly 600) and his unique honor of being named Most Valuable Player in both the National and American Leagues.

But his resourcefulness for knocking down fences wherever he played stands out most of all. Since his career began in 1956, Robinson has homered in 32 different ballparks during regular-season games.

Because Robinson's brilliant career spans two leagues during their era of expansion, franchise shifting and new stadiums, his mark may be difficult to match. However, Leo Cardenas, who once played with Robinson in Cincinnati but never seemed in the same class as a slugger, has come close. Though he has hit only little over 100 homers, he did it in 26 different parks.

Major-league ballparks where Frank Robinson has hit at least one home run in regular-season games:

Anaheim Stadium, Atlanta Stadium, Baltimore Memorial Stadium, Boston Fenway Park, Brooklyn Ebbets Field, Chicago White Sox Park, Chicago Wrigley Field, Cincinnati Crosley Field, Cincinnati Riverfront Stadium, Cleveland Municipal Stadium, Detroit Tiger Stadium, Houston Colt Stadium, Jersey City Roosevelt Park (where the old Brooklyn Dodgers played a few games), Kansas City Municipal Stadium, Kansas City Royals Stadium, Los

Angeles Dodger Stadium, Los Angeles Coliseum, Milwaukee County Stadium, Minnesota Metropolitan Stadium, New York Yankee Stadium, New York Shea Stadium, New York Polo Grounds, Oakland-Alameda County Stadium, Philadelphia Connie Mack Stadium, Philadelphia Veterans Stadium, Pittsburgh Forbes Field, St. Louis Busch Stadium, San Diego Stadium, San Francisco Candlestick Park, San Francisco Seals Stadium, Texas Arlington Stadium, Washington RFK Stadium.

38 Homers That Were Worth Four Home-Run Titles in the Majors

Harry Davis wasn't what you would call a slugger by modern standards. The first baseman for the Philadelphia Athletics at the turn of the century was only 5 feet, 10 inches tall and about 180 pounds. During his 22-year career in the majors, which lasted until 1917, he slammed only 74 homers—a total Hank Aaron or Babe Ruth would collect in a couple of back-to-back bad years. Davis hit home runs at the rate of 1.1

per cent of the times he came to bat, compared to Ruth who got 8.5 homers per 100 at bats.

Furthermore, Davis had to be talked into staying in the majors by the Athletics' Connie Mack in 1901 after bouncing around with four National League teams for five years.

But Davis, a .277 lifetime hitter, made the best of his years. From 1904 through 1907, Davis won the American League's home-run title four straight times—with a *total* of 38 homers.

Davis connected for ten in 1904, eight in 1905, a career high of 12 in 1906 and eight again in 1907, as he dominated the sluggers of his time.

The Father and Son Who Pitched to Ted Williams

Ted Williams' hitting feats smacked of the dramatic. For parts of four different decades, he awed fellow major leaguers with his Herculean hits.

But one family he left a particularly special impression on was Thornton Lee's. Lee was a veteran lefthanded pitcher for the Chicago White

Sox when Williams came up in 1939. Lee lasted 15 years in the American League and thus got a chance to see more than one Williams home run rising over his head while he was on the mound. After all, Williams won four American League home-run titles between 1941 and 1949, despite being away three of those years for military service.

Thornton Lee had a legacy, however.

Don Lee, a righthander pitching for the Washington Senators, was new to the starting rotation just as Williams was bowing out of baseball in 1960.

On September 2 that year, Williams tagged the younger Lee for a homer, too. It was one of the last few of the 521 he smacked in the big leagues—and perhaps the only time major-league home runs were hit by the same man against a father and son.

HITTING FEATS

Five for Five—Swings

Stan Musial's batting feats rank along side of Ted Williams'. It's safe to say that since 1940, they have had no peers.

His career total of 3,630 hits, his seven batting championships, his .376 average in 1948 are testimonials to his greatness. To single out a feat from his 22-year career with the St. Louis Cardinals is a feat in itself.

But that 1948 season, when he was at his best, Stan The Man came through with an incredible performance to maintain his lofty batting average. Three times that season, Musial had gone 5-for-5 at bat. But on September 22, in a game against the league-leading Boston Braves, Musial was in no shape to repeat his five hits in five at-bats.

He had just been hanging in, suffering from an injured wrist as the season was coming to an end.

The batting championship was virtually his, whether he played or not. The next best contender for the title lagged some 40 percentage points behind.

The cold, windy weather that day wasn't in his favor either, but Musial insisted on playing.

On his first time up, he lashed the first pitch for a single.

Next time he came to bat, he doubled on the initial throw.

On his very next time up, he improved his distance hitting by smacking a home run—his 38th of the season. Again he did it on the first pitch.

Musial's left wrist continued to bother him, especially when the lefthanded batter tried to pull the ball.

However, it bothered him only physically. Mentally, Musial couldn't have been sharper. The next time he came to bat, he eyed the first pitch thrown him very carefully and singled again. To cap off the day his fifth (and last) time up, he again singled on the first pitch to come his way.

Dozens upon dozens of players had gone 5-for-5, but none had ever gone 5-for-5 on five pitches!

From 0 Hits in 18 At-Bats to 7-for-7

The heavy hitters in baseball never felt threatened when 155-pound Cesar Gutierrez lugged his 36-ounce bat to the plate during his brief major-league career. There was no way "Cocoa" was going to dislodge any of their records. The only reason he swung the big bat, he had said himself, was to try to knock a few bloopers over infielders' heads.

Cocoa Gutierrez didn't make it to the major leagues for his hitting anyway. The petite Venezuelan was a slick fielding shortstop and utility infielder when he joined the San Francisco Giants in 1967. But his batting was so unimpressive he was shipped to the Detroit Tigers in the American League in 1970. It was there that he finally got a chance—at age twenty-seven—to become a regular in the majors.

Gutierrez started fast with the Tigers, batting .299 after the first few weeks of the season. But just about everyone figured Cocoa was hitting over his head. By mid-June he had settled down to a more realistic .218 and managed to put together a particularly poor string of Sunday afternoon games—with 0 hits in 18 times at bat. Even Cocoa shouldn't have been too disappointed when Manager Mayo Smith benched him in favor of Ken Szotkiewicz for the first game of a Sunday doubleheader against the Cleveland Indians, June 21.

But when the righthanded-hitting Szotkiewicz went hitless in the opening game, the lefthanded-hitting Gutierrez replaced him for the second game.

When Cocoa learned he would be batting against a young lefthanded Cleveland rookie, he brashly told his teammate, slugger Willie Horton, "Watch me get two hits."

Gutierrez got one of those "two hits" in the first inning when he looped a single to centerfield off his rookie opponent, Rick Austin. He also scored the Tigers' initial run. The next time he came to bat was in the third inning and again he tagged Austin for a single—this time a hard drive to centerfield—and again scored a run. It touched off a rally that helped the Tigers narrow the Indians' margin to 6-5 in what was developing as a wide-open game. After the second single, Horton wryly suggested to the little Venezuelan that he ought to get two more hits.

Gutierrez more than took Horton's advice.

Cocoa pushed a drive into the hole between third base and shortstop in the fifth inning against a new Cleveland pitcher and beat out the grounder for another single. In the seventh inning, he punched out a double. In the eighth, he swung his 36-ounce bat and connected solidly for a single that drove in a run to tie the game at 8-all. The tying run was an important one for Gutierrez; it would set him up for an opportunity to make history.

In the twentieth century, no major-league ballplayer had ever gone 7-for-7 in a ballgame, nor had anyone ever gotten seven consecutive hits in the same game. Others had had seven or more hits, but they were interspersed with outs.

The game went into extra innings when neither team scored in the ninth. So up came Gutierrez again, this time with a chance to join those players who had tied the major-league record of 6-for-6. He did, too, with a grounder through the middle of the infield which the Indian shortstop dove for and touched, but couldn't hold. The shortstop recovered the ball but couldn't get to second base in time to make the force out on another Tiger runner, so Cocoa had hit No. 6. The Tigers' batting coach, Wally Moses, who had been working closely with Gutierrez during his slump, informed him that he had some kind of a record.

"I said I'll try for seven," said the surprised hitter, "but never in my life did I ever think of a record."

When both teams went scoreless in that inning and the next, Gutierrez was able to go for the record he hadn't known about. Suddenly the No. 7 uniform he had been issued when he joined the Detroit Tigers was taking on a new meaning.

Phil Hennigan, a Vietnam veteran, was on the mound for the Indians in the twelfth inning when the fledgling record-breaker came up for his final try. He was the fifth pitcher Gutierrez would face that Sunday. Tiger teammate Mickey Stanley had already put Detroit ahead, 9-8, with a home run before Cocoa got to bat, relieving some of the pressure from him. With Hennigan still upset by the shot hit over the centerfield fence, Gutierrez slammed the ball right at the pitcher. It was a hard drive that Gutierrez later would say was his best-hit ball of the day. Hennigan got a glove on it but could not hold it. He searched for the ball and tried to recover it as Gutierrez scrambled for first base. By the time Hennigan made his throw, Cocoa had landed safely on first. There was no question about the drive being a clean hit. No. 7 had made his seventh hit in seven times at bat. The Tigers hung on to win the game.

In one game alone, Gutierrez had raised his batting average a full 31 points, from .218 to .249. He continued to start at shortstop for the Tigers after that in 1970, then lost his job in

Incredible Baseball Feats

Hub (Shucks) Pruett, the St. Louis Browns'
rookie who in 1922 *struck out* Babe Ruth 10
times in the 16 times the mighty Yankee confronted him. *U.P.I.*

Hoyt Wilhelm ended his 21-year career with a record 1,070 appearances as a pitcher. *U.P.I.*

Carl Hubbell of the New York Giants struck out 5
All-Stars in two innings.
Baseball Hall of Fame

On May 13, 1952, Ron Necciai of the Bristol
Twins in the Appalachian League struck out 27
batters in nine innings. *U.P.I.*

In 1956, The Yankees' Don Larsen, who had had a few beers and turned in late the night before, pitched the first no-hitter in World Series history. *U.P.I.*

Frank Robinson, who in 1974 was named baseball's first black manager, holds the unique honor of being named MVP in both the National and American Leagues. He holds another little-known distinction: he has hit home runs in 32 different ballparks in regular-season games. *Baseball Hall of Fame*

Cesar Gutierrez of the Detroit Tigers, the first major-leaguer in the twentieth century to go 7-for-7 in a ballgame—with teammate Al Kaline, who as a 20-year-old won the AL batting championship. *U.P.I.*

Dale Long—the player wh became the first lefthande catcher in the majors sinc 1902. The Pirates though up the idea, but neve played him. Later, Lon caught for the Chicag Cubs. Note the rare lef hander's mitt. *Dale Long*

Bert Campaneris of the A's played all nine positions in one game—September 8, 1965. When Cesar Tovar duplicated the feat in 1968, Campy was proud of him. *U.P.I.*

In 1908, Gabby Street of the Washington Senators,
caught a ball thrown from the top of the Washington
Monument—a feat perhaps topped by Babe Ruth

who is said to have caught the ball tossed from the plane shown in this rare photograph.
Both photos: Baseball Hall of Fame

Fifteen-year-old Joe Nuxhall went from junior high school to the big leagues. At 15, he pitched for the Cincinnati Reds. *U.P.I.*

Warren Spahn's first no-hitter in the majors set a record: at 39, he was the oldest player ever to pitch a major league no-hitter. Six months later, Spahn saw the record re-written—by 40-year-old Warren Spahn's second no-hitter. *U.P.I.*

Satchel Paige, at 62 years of age, was on the roster of the Atlanta Braves. *U.P.I.*

Roy McMillan, who signed a big-league contract before he had ever played a game of baseball.
Baseball Hall of Fame

Bobo Newsome played for 18 different teams, inclu
nine big-league clubs. He is the only twentieth cen
200-game winner to lose more than he won (211-2
and lead the AL in losses four times—a record.
Baseball Hall of Fame

Pete (One-Arm) Gray, once voted MVP of the Sout!
Association, played with the St. Louis Browns, for a w
pennant-chasing season. *Baseball Hall of Fame, U.F*

1971 to a .228 hitter. Soon after, he was out of the majors.

The final irony of the story of No. 7 was that he only wore his lucky number by a fluke. In 1968, following the premature death of Tiger Manager Charlie Dressan, who wore No. 7, the number was temporarily retired. For no reason at all, it was brought out again by the equipment manager when Gutierrez joined the team.

Big-league baseball's only other 7-for-7 occurred before there even was an American League. It happened on June 10, 1892, when Baltimore had a National League franchise.

That day, in a game against St. Louis, the old Baltimore Orioles got hot and everybody but the pitcher was getting two or more hits. St. Louis' pitching staff was having a terrible day holding down the Baltimore bats, perhaps because one of its hurlers was a youngster making his first and only major-league appearance, and another was only a couple of years removed from the semi-pro ranks.

Baltimore had 25 runs by the end of the sixth inning.

Leading the Oriole attack was its catcher, Wilbert Robinson, an unimposing hitter batting eighth in the order. The short, robust Robinson, a lifetime .273 hitter, found the range against St. Louis. He bopped six singles and a double in seven times at bat for the first and only 7-for-7 day until Gutierrez came along eight decades later. Unlike Gutierrez, Robinson collected his seven hits in nine innings.

Strangely enough, Robinson's feat went unnoticed for almost two decades. It wasn't until Robinson, by then a big-league manager, mentioned it to a sportswriter in 1912 that the record day was given any newspaper reviews. In 1892 it wasn't reported at all except in the box score.

The most hits in a single game?

It happened in 1932, when shortstop John Burnett of the Cleveland Indians lashed out seven singles and two doubles in nine times at bat on July 10. However, the hits were not consecutive during the 18-inning game.

Like Gutierrez, Burnett played only one year as a major-league regular.

16 Times on Base in 16 Trips to the Plate

Ted Williams had just passed his thirty-ninth birthday in late August of 1957 but he still was the most dangerous batter in baseball. That year the Boston Red Sox outfielder batted .388—the closest any major leaguer has come to hitting .400 since Williams himself achieved that figure in 1941.

But shortly after Williams reached age thirty-nine, he was forced to sit out a couple of weeks due to illness.

He was still too weak to play full time when he came back to the team on September 17. That didn't stop him from slugging a pinch-hit home run, though.

The next day, Williams got into a game again as a pinch hitter and was walked. In another pinch situation two days later, he homered again.

Healthy enough to play full time again, he was back in the starting lineup on September 20. He celebrated his return by getting on base each time he went to bat. In the first of those at-bats he was walked. After homering the next time up, he was walked twice.

On September 22, he started again. And once more he got on base each time he went to bat. First came a walk, then a home run (which gave him four straight homers in official at-bats). He singled his third time up, then was walked again. Williams had now reached base 11 straight times.

Even at thirty-nine, Williams remained the most feared batter in baseball, which was the reason for all the walks. In 1957 alone, he was intentionally walked 33 times for the official record (though Babe Ruth fans claim their man was passed intentionally as many as 80 times in a season).

On September 23, Williams was back on base again. He singled his first time up, then was walked three more times. In his fifth at-bat, Williams was hit by a pitched ball.

He had come to bat 16 times since sitting out two weeks because of illness and each time he reached base successfully. It is a record that still stands. But then, Ted Williams was expected to set records that would stand the test of time.

Third baseman Tommy Brown of the Nashville Vols of the Southern Association probably holds the all-time professional record for getting on base in successive at-bats.

In May of 1956, Brown had a string of 10 hits and six bases on balls before going into a game with the Birmingham Barons. The Barons chose to walk him four times rather than pitch to him—so Brown stretched his on-base streak to 20. His last time up, he flied out.

The Team With Seven .300 Hitters in the Lineup

Their batting order was an imposing one, and certainly one of the greatest ever in baseball for a single season. For example, the 1930 Philadelphia Phillies often fielded a team with *seven* .300 hitters in the lineup at one time. And they weren't cheap .300 hitters, either.

In the outfield were Chuck Klein (.386), Lefty O'Doul (.383) and Don Hurst (.327) or Barney Friberg (.341). Third baseman Pinky Whitney batted .342 that year. Part-time first baseman Monk Sherlock, who shared his position with Hurst, batted .324. The platooning catchers, Harry McCurdy and Spud Davis, hit .331 and .313, respectively. Shortstop Tommy Thevenow

batted .286 and his keystone mate, second baseman Fresco Thompson, hit .282. By today's
standards, Thevenow and Thompson would gain
the respect of the finest pitchers.

As a ballclub that season, the powerful Phillies
averaged .315 at bat.

And what did such fine hitting get the Phillies?

Not much. That year, they finished a dead last
in the eight-team National League—a full 40 games
behind first place!

Seems that the '30 Phillies liked to give better
than receive. Despite scoring 994 runs, the Phillies gave up a whopping 1,199 while losing 102
of 154 games.

There was an explanation for the Phillies'
strange success/failure story. The National League
had a hopped ball in play that season. Six of
eight teams batted over .300 and the other two
bettered the .280 mark. The league-leading St.
Louis Cardinals alone had eleven .300 hitters and
the New York Giants set the all time major-league
record by batting .319 as a unit. A 4.07 earned
run average got a man fifth place in the National
League pitching statistics.

The following season, the zip was taken out of
the ball and no one in the National League batted over .350. No team batted over .289. The

Phillies in 1931? They fell off 36 points as a team at bat—and gained two notches in the standings.

The last of the .300-hitting teams was the 1950 Boston Red Sox of the American League. The Bosox, featuring Ted Williams (.317), Billy Goodman (.354), Dom DiMaggio (.328), Al Zarilla (.325), Walt Dropo (.322) and others, averaged .302 for the season. Red Sox players crossed the plate over 1,000 times in 154 games.

And what did the Red Sox get for their efforts?

A third-place finish in an eight-team league.

Driving the Opposition Batty

The most runs batted in during a single game by a major leaguer is 12, a record established back in 1924 by the St. Louis Cardinals' clean-up batter, Jim Bottomley. Tony Lazzeri of the New York Yankees, another cleanup hitter, set the American League mark with 11, thanks to two grand slammers, in a 1936 game. And minor leaguers have gotten as many as 16 in a single contest.

Thus at first glance the 11 RBI's collected in one game by collegian Dave Stegman in 1974 seems minute.

The University of Arizona outfielder knocked in that many for what was thought to be a collegiate record (NCAA, at least) against the University of Texas-El Paso.

He doubled in a run in the second inning, socked an opposite field homer with the bases loaded in the third, tripled in two more runs in the fourth, singled in one in the sixth, then capped his performance with a bases-loaded triple in the ninth as his team won, 27-6.

If Stegman was no Bottomley or a Lazzeri, he could boast that his feat was distinct in one respect—he was Arizona's leadoff man at the time.

PLAYING THE FIELD

Two Players With "Nine Lives"

Most baseball players enjoy the security of playing only one position. It's healthier for the batting average, they figure, and other times it's just healthier being adjusted to balls coming only from one direction.

But Bert Campaneris decided to be more game than his big-league counterparts near the end of the 1965 American League campaign. His Kansas City A's were struggling along in last place, trying to evoke some interest before they moved on to a new home in Oakland, California. Throughout most of 1965, Campaneris, the spirited base runner, was all there was to cheer about.

As a rookie in 1964, Campaneris had played shortstop, third base and the outfield in an effort to establish a position. The twenty-two-year-old Cuban was definitely big-league material. It was just a matter of where to put him so that he could go about the business of generating some offense.

By 1965, he was set at shortstop, where he would become outstanding.

But when the crowds dwindled late in the season, Campaneris and the A's unconventional owner, Charley O. Finley, came up with a gimmick to draw some fans. Campaneris would attempt to become the first man in modern baseball history to play every position—and do it in one game.

Charley Finley took out a million-dollar insurance policy on Campaneris for September 8. Then Campy Campaneris Night was proclaimed publicly, and Finley took out advertisements in local newspapers to bellow out Campaneris' bold adventurous attempt. It was rumored that Finley also slipped Campaneris a few extra dollars for the announced attraction.

Campaneris deserved it. Over 21,000 fans came out for the game at Kansas City's municipal Stadium to see if Campy could play all nine positions against the California Angels.

Campaneris opened the game at his usual position—shortstop. He didn't field a ball.

In the next inning he moved to second base and got an assist when he ran down a trapped baserunner.

In Inning No. 3, Campy played third and didn't have to budge.

Then he moved to each of the outfield positions for innings 4, 5 and 6. He caught fly balls in left and center but dropped a wind-blown fly in right that cost the A's a run. He was charged with an error.

In the seventh inning, Campaneris moved to first base. At 5 feet 10 inches and 160 pounds, he hardly could pass for the tall, well-built sluggers who usually get that chore. But he held his own and caught an infield popup.

It was over to the pitching mound in the eighth inning of what had developed into a tight 2-1 game, the Angels leading. But Campy got his cousin, José Cardenal, out on a pop fly. However, he walked the next two men on eight straight pitches, then got nipped for a single that drove in a run. He did strike out Bobby Knoop, a .269 hitter. And he got out of the inning with no further damage when a base runner was thrown out trying to steal.

The biggest test, according to Campaneris, came in the ninth when he moved in behind the plate to catch. That's why he saved it for last.

The first man up for the Angels, 200-pound Ed Kirkpatrick, singled and stole second on Campaneris. The next man walked and the following player flied out with Kirkpatrick moving to third.

With a man on first and third, the Angels decided to try a double steal on the raw recruit behind the plate. Campaneris threw to his second baseman Dick Green, who quickly relayed the ball back home to catch the charging Kirkpatrick. Campaneris took Green's throw while he was standing on the third base line a few feet in front of the plate. Kirkpatrick had only one chance—to knock the ball out of Campaneris' hands. So he barreled into him and knocked him to the ground. Campaneris bravely held onto the ball for the out. Then, like a good tough catcher, he went to battle with Kirkpatrick.

The insurance company got a slight scare out of the ordeal, because Campaneris was carted off to a local hospital for X-rays of his shoulder. But he proved to be okay.

Offensively, Campaneris went hitless. He picked up his 49th steal of the year and scored a run after a walk in the first inning. But then he wasn't out to prove anything on offense that night.

Cesar Tovar of the Minnesota Twins was almost better suited for the record attempt in 1965. The rookie American Leaguer had played four positions that season for the Twins—second, third, short and the outfield—even though he played in only 18 games.

When he made his 1968 attempt to match Campaneris' feat, he had played six different positions in the big leagues. The only ones he hadn't tried beforehand were pitcher, catcher and first base. And he had played the other six positions extensively, depending on where manager Cal Ermer needed him.

A good hitter, Tovar didn't seem to be bothered by switching around, though he once said he would prefer rightfield if he had a choice.

By September of 1968, he had switched positions some 40 times during the season. And he only made three errors. At bat, the little 155-pound Venezuelan kept his average in the .280 range.

So on September 22, he was prepared for a nine-position night. The opponent was the Oakland A's—featuring Bert Campaneris.

Tovar bravely started out on the mound. The first man he faced was, appropriately, Bert Campaneris. Tovar got him out on a foul ball to third. Next came powerful Reggie Jackson. Tovar struck him out after a full count. Danny Cater walked and went to second on a balk, but Tovar survived the inning by getting Sal Bando to foul out.

Tovar proudly wore a jacket on the walk in from the bullpen, as all pitchers do, and made use of the resin bag. He did suffer from a sore arm the next day, though, and it was directly attributed to his no-hit pitching stint.

Next inning, Tovar was behind the plate in another show of strength. His equipment wasn't up to par, but he held onto a third strike, kept two base runners in check, and even made a trip to the mound to confer with his pitcher.

Making History with Campy

California	AB	R	H	RBI
Cardenal, cf	6	0	0	1
Pearson, lf	5	2	1	0
Fregosi, ss	5	1	1	0
Adcock, 1b	4	0	2	2
Lopez, pr	0	0	0	0
Power, 1b	0	0	0	0
Smith, ph	1	0	0	0
Dees, 1b	1	0	0	0
Knoop, 2b	3	1	1	0
Kirkpatrick, rf	5	0	2	0
Egan, c	2	0	0	0
Rodgers, c	2	1	0	0
Schaal, 3b	5	0	1	0
Chance, p	4	0	0	0
Lee, p	1	0	0	0
Ranew, ph	1	0	0	0
Totals	45	5	8	3

Kansas City	AB	R	H	RBI
Campaneris, ss-2b-3b-lf-cf-rf-1b-c-p	3	1	0	0
Lachemann, c	2	0	2	0
Tartabull, cf-rf	4	0	0	0
Causey, 2b-ss	5	1	2	0
Charles, 3b-2b	6	0	1	1
Landis, cf-rf	5	1	1	0
Bryan, c	3	0	1	0
Harrelson, ph	1	0	1	1
Talbot, pr	0	0	0	0
Reynolds, ph	1	0	0	0
Blanchard, ph	1	0	0	0
Schwartz, 1b	2	0	0	0
Hershberger, rf	0	0	0	0
Stahl, rf	3	0	0	0

Playing the Field

Kansas City	AB	R	H	RBI
Clinton, rf	1	0	0	0
Green, 2b	4	0	1	1
Joyce, p	2	0	0	0
Rosario, 1b	3	0	0	0
Totals	46	3	9	3

California	0 0 0	1 0 1	0 1 0	0 0 0	2—5
Kansas City	1 0 0	0 0 0	0 0 2	0 0 0	0—3

California	IP	H	R	ER	BB	SO
Chance	8⅓	5	3	3	2	6
Lee (W. 9-6)	3⅔	4	0	0	3	1
Coates (Save No. 1)	1	0	0	0	0	0

Kansas City	IP	H	R	ER	BB	SO
Joyce	6*	5	2	1	1	2
Mossi	⅓	0	0	0	0	0
Dickson	⅔	0	0	0	1	1
Campaneris	1	1	1	1	2	1
Monteagudo	1	1	0	0	1	1
Wyatt	2	1	0	0	2	0
O'Donoghue (L. 8-18) ..	1†	0	2	0	1	0
Segui	1	0	0	0	1	0

*Faced one batter in seventh.

†Faced three batters in the thirteenth.

E—Campaneris, Causey, O'Donoghue. DP—Kansas City 1. LOB—California 12, Kansas City 10. 2B—Charles, Adcock, Bryan. SB—Campaneris, Kirkpatrick, Tartabull. SH—Tartabull, Kirkpatrick. SF—Cardenal. HBP—By Chance (Landis). WP—Dickson. PB—Egan. T—4:14. A—21,576.

From then on, Tovar went around the horn—
playing first, second, short and third for an inning
each. There were no disasters. He had an assist at
first and a putout at second. Then came the outfield positions that were natural to him. He made
two catches in left and one in center. All in all, he
handled six chances and handled them well, and
retired as a no-hit pitcher. Bert Campaneris was
proud of him.

The World Series Unassisted Triple Play

The fans at the Cleveland Indian-Brooklyn
Dodger World Series game on October 10, 1920,
were being treated to more than their share of
Series history. Indian rightfielder Elmer Smith
smacked a grand-slam home run in the first inning—it was the first such slam in Series history.
Then Indian pitcher Jim Bagby slugged one out of
the park in the third inning to become the first
pitcher to get a four-bagger in Series play. The
game was becoming a rout, much to the pleasure
of the hometown Indian fans. As it turned out,

the Dodgers would out-hit the Indians that day, 13-12, and still lose, 8-1.

But the best fireworks of the game were still to come. In the fifth inning, the Dodgers started getting to Bagby, a 31-game winner that season. There were no outs and two men on—Otto Miller at first and Pete Kilduff at second—when Clarence Mitchell came to bat for Brooklyn in the fifth. Mitchell was a pretty good hitting pitcher who had come in to relieve the Dodger starter just the inning before.

Bill Wambsganss was settled in his position as the husky left-handed hitter dug in at the plate to face Jim Bagby.

Then it happened—"All in a flash," recalled Wambsganss, the veteran infielder who lasted 13 years in the majors because of his catlike defense.

Mitchell drove a hard liner toward right-center. Luckily for Wambsganss, it came right to him. Kilduff and Miller took off with the shot of the ball; to them, it could not have seemed anything but a long hit.

But Wambsganss speared the drive out of the air as the base runners raced head down to scoring positions.

Wambsganss rushed to second, where he retired Kilduff by stepping on base. By now, Miller was nearing second and had not yet grasped the situation. For some reason, Miller kept coming at Wambsganss instead of making the turn and trying to get back to first. Wambsganss tagged him out.

He had performed baseball's rare unassisted triple play under World Series conditions. Within a matter of five or six seconds, the meek-hitting second baseman with a flair for fielding had etched his name into baseball's archives.

Wambsganss often reminded others that he could have missed his coveted spot in history.

"A few feet one way or another and it would have been a safe hit," he said. "It came to me like a shot, high in the air, so I reached for it, grabbed it and held it. As for Miller, he could have turned. He wouldn't have made it but he would have caused me to throw (to first) and lose the unassisted triple play."

There have been only eight unassisted triple plays in big league history—five by shortstops and two by first basemen. All came with men on first and second. Wambsganss was the only second baseman ever to make the astonishing play.

But according to Wambsganss, a second baseman just missed on another occasion. The near-miss performer was Wambsganss himself.

He told of the time, in a game against the old St. Louis Browns, when he speared a line drive, tagged out a man who had just left second, and then began to chase down a slow-footed Brown who was headed back to first base. Wambsganss ran after him until the final moment, then felt obligated to make the throw to nail the runner.

Not one to rest on the glory of the moment he made Series, and baseball, history, Wambsganss once admitted: "Almost every game I played after that, I had in mind the possibility of making such a play."

Tinkers-to-Evers-to-Chance was a double-play combination so exciting it was immortalized by a very famous verse.

Heffner-to-somebody-to-somebody got lost in history. But the Welch, W. Va., Miners of the Appalachian League had a combination that for one day made the old Chicago Cub threesome look like shortcut artists.

In the seventh inning of a July 26, 1954, game against Johnson City, third baseman Lee Heffner scooped up a grounder with runners on first and second and tagged the base in front of him for a quick out. Then he tossed the ball to his second baseman for another out and the second sacker tossed it to first for the triple play.

That wasn't uncommon, but when Heffner snared a line drive in the next inning and threw the ball to second, and the second baseman relayed it on to first for another triple play, the Welch Miners had dug out a feat that may never have been made before. Baseball historians could find no other instances of back-to-back triple plays in consecutive innings.

The Outfielder's Triple Play

The rare unassisted triple play usually takes place when a shortstop, a second baseman or a first baseman—all of whom are in the middle of the action when a line drive goes whistling through the air with at least two men on base—snags the hard-hit ball, steps on a base and catches a runner coming in from another base at a point where it is too late for him to turn around.

The components of the unassisted triple play then are usually a well-hit drive, an alert infielder and base runners of exceptional speed or with a long lead off base. Only eight unassisted plays have occurred in big-league baseball and few are accomplished in the minors.

But Walter Carlisle of the Vernon team (based in Los Angeles) of the Pacific Coast League added a footnote to fielding history during a game played July 19, 1911. Vernon was playing the Los Angeles club.

With the score tied in the ninth inning, and

men on first and second with none out, Los Angeles signaled for the hit-and-run.

As the Los Angeles batter swung, Carlisle edged in from his position in centerfield until he was almost near second base.

In one of the quickest swoops ever seen on a baseball field, Carlisle grabbed a line drive, somersaulted, landed on his feet, tagged second base for out No. 2, and ran to first base before the baserunner could get back for out No. 3. Carlisle, a centerfielder, had performed a feat no other professional baseball player ever had—an unassisted triple play by an outfielder!

Lest some other outfielder thinks he can match Carlisle's feat, he must remember that there was something special about the Vernon player—he was an ex-circus acrobat.

A Lefthanded Catcher in the Majors

It was the second or third day of spring practice in San Bernardino, Calif., for the Pittsburgh Pirates in 1951 when Manager Billy Meyer approached rookie first baseman Dale Long to inform him that the team's general manager, Branch Rickey, wanted to try him out as a catcher. Long was game for the experiment—"I'd have done anything, even run through brick walls, to make the majors," he said—but he felt he should remind the manager of one thing: he was a lefthanded thrower. Meyer's initial reaction was to take out a copy of the roster with its pertinent physical characteristics and read it in front of Long. "By God, you *are* a lefty," said Meyer.

Before sending Long behind the plate, Meyer felt obligated to contact Rickey, an ex-catcher himself, and let him know the surprising information he had just learned. The astute Rickey's answer was typical: "Judas Priest, Billy, that's what I want—a lefthanded catcher."

Rickey, the pioneer who introduced vast farm systems and Jackie Robinson to organized baseball, had done it again. He would try to introduce the first lefthanded catcher to the majors since 1902.

Long was a fast, home-run-hitting twenty-five-year-old with impressive size. He was 6 feet, 4 inches tall and weighed about 200 pounds. Why Rickey singled him out for the experiment, Long never knew. But he gave it his best. Each day, he'd get up earlier than the other players and catch 200 balls tossed at him by Iron Mike, the pitching machine. Long had a morning companion—a young player Rickey was trying to switch from a righthanded batter to a lefthander. The prospect had struck out 195 times the previous season.

They made for an odd couple. Long would work all morning with Iron Mike and his wild swinging companion, play four or five innings of an exhibition game behind the plate, then return to the pitching machine for more practice late in the afternoon. But the great experiment fizzled and Long never did catch for the Pirates. He went on to earn his fame in another fashion, slugging home runs in eight straight games as a first baseman.

"I kept a lefthanded catcher's mitt around, though," he recalled. But the only use it got was in the dugout where Dale used it as a cushion.

Then one day in 1958, when he didn't have his special mitt anymore, Long was summoned to catch. He was playing for the Chicago Cubs that season. Cal Neeman, the Cubs' regular catcher, was ejected from the game. His backup had pinch hit earlier in the day, so he too was out of the game. Manager Bob Scheffing pleaded with the umpire, but to no avail. "That's your problem," he was told.

Scheffing, an ex-catcher, apparently had heard of the Long experiment. He called on his slugging first baseman to fill in behind the plate that August day against the Philadelphia Phillies. Long donned all the catching gear except for a mitt. He had to use his first baseman's glove.

Long toiled behind the plate for the rest of that inning, plus another one. Despite the lack of glove and preparation, there were no major disasters. But the next day, a Cub representative was dispatched to the Chicago-based Wilson Sporting Goods Company to purchase an emergency supply of lefthanded catcher's mitts. A month later, in another emergency situation against the Los Angeles Dodgers, Long filled in for a short stretch and again avoided any catastrophes. Twice that season he made history. First, he may have been the only major leaguer to go behind the plate without a catcher's mitt. Then he became the only player in modern history to catch with a lefthanded mitt. No one has duplicated his experiences.

Why haven't there been other lefthanded catchers?

Probably because there have been no other Branch Rickeys. Baseball is wedded to its traditions and a lefthanded catcher is just too much to get used to.

For Dale Long, there were some definite problems. Many of them had to do with pitchers not being able to adjust. The hurlers just could not get used to the vision of a catcher's mitt protruding from the opposite side of the plate.

Years later, however, Long admitted there

were some personal areas of difficulty as well. "We really do live in a righthander's world," he said. For some reason that he couldn't explain—and he was a pretty good student of the game—it was more difficult for a lefthander to make the throw to second base. He said that the lefthander's throw had a sideways spin that made it "sail" during the 127-foot toss. Because the throw drifted away from second, Long had to make adjustments to lead the throw.

His toughest situation, however, was an opponent stealing third when a righthanded pitcher was on the mound and a lefthanded batter was at the plate. "You had to turn your whole body away from the movement when that happened," he recalled.

As for stepping in behind the plate in an emergency, Long had no real problem with signs. "I just used the 1-2-3 system," he said. "One finger for a fastball, two for a curve, three for a change of speed and I wiggled one for a changeup." Making history was as simple as that.

Rifle Arms

Baseball scouts get fascinated by the throwing arms of the prospects they are checking out. But players are careful not to test their arms for distance throwing too often for fear of injury.

Throughout the years, though, some players have taken up the challenge to see just who is the longest thrower—for distance. For years, that distinction belonged to an ex-minor leaguer named Sheldon LeJeune. In an exhibition at Cincinnati in 1910, LeJeune tossed a ball 426 feet, 9½ inches. He had just completed his season with Evansville of the Central League.

LeJeune saw his record stand for 42 years. It wasn't until September 7, 1952, that another minor leaguer—Don Grate, who played for Chattanooga of the Southern Association—outdistanced him. Grate threw a ball 434 feet, 1 inch.

But even Grate's mark was not out of reach for another rifle arm—ex-big-league outfielder Glen Gorbous.

Gorbous had played briefly and without distinction with the Cincinnati Reds and Philadelphia Phillies in 1955 and 1956. The lanky 6-foot, 2-inch Canadian just wasn't up to major-league standards as a hitter. But he could throw.

He proved that in the 1957 season when he played for a minor-league team in Omaha of the American Association.

In a pre-planned exhibition on August 1, Gorbous made four throws from the rightfield corner at Omaha Stadium to the leftfield corner. For each attempt, he would get a six-step running start. Aided by a slight 3-mph tailwind, Gorbous made one throw that was measured at 445 feet, 10 inches. It's still the record to beat.

Catching a "High and Outside" One

Babe Ruth and Gabby Street were two baseball players who reached their peaks in big-league games. But the real "height" of their careers came off the field. In fact, Street probably got more notoriety from an off-field antic than he ever did for his fine catching with the Washington Senators.

On the morning of August 21, 1908, Street went out to the Washington Monument. He would attempt what would be a monumental catch—a baseball dropped from the top floor of that landmark. Street's friend, Preston Gibson, had made a $500 bet that the Senator catcher could catch a ball dropped from the 555-foot high window at the top of the monument. Gibson and his challenger ascended to the top of the building with a basket full of baseballs and a wooden chute-like device that would send the balls sailing off away from the structure. Street was at the ground level, waiting for their first drop.

Gibson sent ten balls down the chute in his quest to give Street a fair chance. But none seemed to clear the side of the building. So the chute was put aside and Gibson started throwing the balls out of the little window. Three throws later, Street scrambled around on the ground and made his historic catch. He admitted later that he couldn't see the balls until they were halfway down. He also said the wind hindered him.

Scientists have estimated that the ball had a force of some 200 to 300 pounds at the time Street got a mitt on it.

Though Street got most of the publicity for making a high catch, he wasn't the only person to reach such heights. Thirty years later, two Cleveland Indian catchers—Frankie Pytlak and Hank Helf—caught balls dropped from the 710-foot level of Terminal Tower in Cleveland. Another Cleveland player named Joe Sprinz performed the greatest stunt catch, though, when he took in a ball dropped 800 feet from an airship in 1931. The record-holder paid for his catch: as the force of the catch broke his jaw.

The common thinking that modern ball-players shouldn't try such freak stunts because it isn't worth the risk to their well-paid careers may have been debunked when the Baseball Hall of Fame received some rare Babe Ruth photos in the 1970s. One photo showed the Babe chasing around in an open field in an attempt to get a ball dropped from a double-winged plane (see photo section). Legend has it that the Babe made the catch.

THE YOUNG
AND THE OLD

Late But Great

Thirty-nine is an age when most major-league baseball players are retired. But when pitcher Warren Spahn reached that milestone in 1960 the only retiring he was doing was to enemy batsmen. At thirty-nine, Spahn was not merely going strong, he was going very strong.

The season was coming to a close on September 16 when the Milwaukee Braves were scheduled to pitch Spahn against the hapless, last-place Philadelphia Phillies. It would be a good opportunity for Spahn to pick up his 20th victory for the fifth year in a row. That is, if he hadn't lost his fastball—as some newspaper accounts had indicated. Undoubtedly, the critics were influenced by his slow start. He was 4-4 in late June.

In fact, lanky Warren Spahn had been a late starter in the big leagues. He pitched a dozen or so innings for the old Boston Braves in 1942 but did not earn a decision. That had to wait until 1946, when he came back from World War II. Spahn was twenty-five before he got his first major-league victory. Contrast that to, say, a pitcher like Dennis McLain, who had already reached the 100-victory mark at age twenty-five.

Spahn may have started late but his records are many. A fiercely competitive player who once posted a 23-7 record after tearing up his knee cartilage in spring training, Spahn is regarded by many as the greatest lefthanded pitcher of all time. In 1960 he was going after his 11th season with 20 or more victories and no one was about to stop him.

But for all his records, Spahn had never thrown a no-hitter in the majors. That was an omission for a man with 286 victories up to that time.

Was it a jinx?

Spahn apparently didn't think so.

On September 16, before the second smallest crowd in Milwaukee's major-league history, Spahn went to the mound and began making up for lost time.

He set down one Phillie after another, and surprisingly with a fastball that was blazing. He was throwing few pitches and very few balls. It was obvious to the 6,117 fans who did show up that he had his stuff this night.

In the fifth inning, Spahn decided to lessen the tension that was beginning to build. As he returned to the dugout after setting down the Phils in order, he said loud enough for his team-mates to hear, "All right, just nobody say I got a no-hitter going." He smiled.

Spahn kept pitching flawless baseball inning after inning. Going into the ninth inning, he hadn't even been ruffled by a Phillie hitter. He had only given up two walks and his strikeout count was reaching his personal best for nine innings.

The first two batters in the final inning were pinch hitters. Spahn disposed of them and collected his 15th strikeout—a personal high in a regulation-length game.

Then came his first challenge of the night.

Bob Malkmus, an infielder with a nondescript batting history, stretched Spahn to the full count. Then on a seventh pitch, Malkmus lined a drive straight at Spahn. Warren got a glove on it through pure luck, then lost the ball when it trickled away. As Spahn searched the infield for the ball, shortstop Johnny Logan raced in, picked up the ball and tossed it to first. Fortunately, Joe Adcock, a 6-foot, 4-inch man, was playing first. He needed all the stretch he could get out of his body to take Logan's low, wide throw. Adcock made a backhanded stab at the ball and got it in time.

Warren Spahn finally had his no-hitter. Never had a player so old accomplished as much in nine big-league innings.

Spahn's record didn't last for long, though. About six months later, a forty-year-old lefthander pitching against the San Francisco Giants only five days after his birthday hurled a no-hit game. Warren Spahn had done it again.

Spahn's ageless performances didn't end with the second no-hitter. He continued to win until he reached 363 victories, then went to the minor leagues at age 45 to try for a comeback. Along with his no-hitters, his other great late accomplishment came in 1963 when he was 42. That year, Spahn won 23 games and pitched seven shutouts, both matching his personal bests as a big leaguer. It was the 13th time he won 20 games or more.

From Junior High to the Majors—In One Step

Major-league baseball didn't have a big-league look about it in 1944. Most of the bright young talents were off to war, and baseball had to settle for the leftovers. Of 400 major leaguers that year, some 157 of them were classified 4-F (physical rejects) by the United States military forces. Many of the rest who filled up big-league rosters were old men—or teenagers.

Typical of the desperate teams was Cincinnati. The Reds were in the National League pennant race early in the season, but were losing players left and right to the military. The Reds, like other teams, were grabbing anybody who moved and putting him on the roster. Scouts were combing the sandlot leagues for instant major-league players.

It was on one such scouting trip to Hamilton, Ohio, that the Reds scout found a strong-armed youngster named Joe Nuxhall. Actually, the scout had made the trip to Hamilton to take a look at Joe's father. He came away more impressed by the boy. Joe Nuxhall's father had been grooming the son for baseball for years. The father used to have the boy throw chunks of coal at a spot on a silo after they unloaded trucks. "I could throw hard," said Nuxhall about his early pitching. "But I didn't know where it was going."

In June of 1944, "it" was going right to the major leagues.

Nuxhall was just a junior-high-school student—fifteen years old. But the Reds offered him $500 to sign a contract and $175 a month, and he grabbed it.

On June 10—when Joe was 15 years, 10 months and 11 days old—he found himself pitching against the league-leading St. Louis Cardinals at Cincinnati's Crosley Field.

Nuxhall had been brought right into the majors along with an eighteen- and a nineteen-year-old. Manager Bill McKechnie was hard pressed for pitchers so he was willing to look at anyone who could throw the ball. The lean lefthanded teenager fit that category.

The Cardinals were leading in the June 10 game, 7-0, when McKechnie pulled his starter, a youngster he had just brought up from the Syracuse farm team on trial (the youngster lasted two days). McKechnie replaced him with a third baseman who had been converted into a pitcher. As the game progressed, the ex-third baseman didn't fare too well, either. He too was replaced, when the score reached 13-0. The manager summoned Nuxhall.

"I thought Mr. McKechnie was kidding," the boyish pitcher recalled. So did the 3,500 fans. But he wasn't.

Nuxhall was visibly shaken when he reached the mound. But somehow he got the first batter to ground out, shortstop to first. He walked the next man, then threw a wild pitch while in the process of getting the third batter to pop out.

Then the roof fell in.

Nuxhall walked another batter, gave up a single, and walked three more. Runs were pouring across the plate and the Reds were heading for the worst defeat by a major-league team in nearly 40 years. Joe got the ninth batter he faced to a 3-2 count, then lost him with a single. He had given up four runs and had men on base when he was replaced.

The Reds eventually lost, 18-0.

Nuxhall went back to high school after that and became a star athlete in basketball and football. But he also continued in professional baseball, too.

The road back to the majors was a tough one for Nuxhall. There were stopovers at several minor-league towns, a series of temper tantrums to overcome and a control problem. One season in the minors, he walked 151 batters in 186 innings.

But the Reds stood patiently behind him and in 1952 he rejoined the team. He was now twenty-four years old.

Nuxhall went on to play 15 more years in the majors, all but one with the Reds. He finished with 135 victories and a 3.90 earned run average overall. The career ERA was a marked improvement over that first season in the majors. After his two-thirds of an inning against the Cardinals, he had posted a 67.50 ERA.

Fifteen years after his disastrous start at Crosley Field, Nuxhall found himself in another bases loaded situation. He was pitching again at Crosley, this time against the Milwaukee Braves. In one inning, Nuxhall fanned dangerous Eddie Mathews and Joe Adcock. Then when he struck out Del Crandall, another slugger, his catcher dropped the ball. Crandall made it to first base to load the bases.

This time, though, Nuxhall held his cool. The next man up was Johnny Logan. Nuxhall struck him out, too—giving the pitcher a rare four-strike-out inning. Only two other pitchers before him had accomplished the feat in the twentieth century.

Recent research by the Baseball Hall of Fame in Cooperstown, New York, indicates that Nuxhall may not have been the youngest major leaguer after all. A player named Fred Chapman took part in a game in 1887 for Philadelphia of the American Association, which was then a major league. Chapman's birthdate has been recorded as November 25, 1872, which would have made him only fourteen years old during the summer of 1887.

But the youngest player ever to take part in a professional game may have been twelve-year-old Joe Relford, of Statesboro, Ga. It happened in 1952.

The fans hollered to the visiting Fitzgerald team, "Put in the batboy!" and manager Charlie Ridgeway obliged. His team was down 13-0 and playing terrible ball in the eighth inning. Ridgeway got the go-ahead from the umpire and inserted Relford in the lineup. He first pinch hit, grounding hard to third base, then served a hitch in centerfield. Relford made a fine stab of a long line drive during the game. For good measure, Joe Relford, who was black, integrated the Class D Georgia State League for the first time.

The incident didn't go over in the league office, though. The manager was suspended, the umpire fired and the batboy dismissed.

The 14-Year-Old Pro

The scheduled 7:30 P.M. minor-league baseball game between Auburn and Batavia in the New York-Penn League had to be moved up to 6 P.M. on August 10, 1974, due to unforeseen circumstances. The hometown Auburn, N. Y., Phillies didn't want to get into trouble with the law.

What Auburn was being careful about was the New York State child labor laws. The statutes read that an employee under sixteen years could not work after 7 P.M. At the time, Auburn was trying to work fourteen-year-old Jorge Lebron into his first professional game, a debut that would make history. Lebron, a shortstop from Puerto Rico, was about to become the youngest player ever to sign a contract and participate in an organized baseball game.

The 5-foot, 10-inch, 150-pounder eventually did play, and he certainly didn't embarrass the people who took a chance on him. On the first pitch of the game, a Batavia player smacked the ball down the middle of the infield. Lebron dashed over, scooped it off the ground and made a successful long throw to first base. He looked like a real pro.

Lebron made another assist, a putout and drew a walk as leadoff man for his team during a three-inning stint.

Lebron had signed with the Philadelphia Phillie farm club in July after a scout in Puerto Rico spotted him and convinced the Phillies to take a chance on him, despite his age. Because Puerto Rican players do not fall within the framework of the major-league player draft, Lebron signed as a free agent. The general manager of the Auburn club was designated the teenager's legal guardian.

Lebron starred in his second game, too. Though he went hitless in four trips to the plate, he made a shoestring catch of one blooper and snagged a line drive, to the delight of 3,642 fans who packed into Auburn's 3,500-seat stadium for a game against Newark. Ironically, Auburn lost the game on errors in extra innings—long after slick-fielding Lebron left the game.

Lebron's brief 1974 season came to an end after that game. He had to return to Puerto Rico to enroll in junior high school.

Someone Old, Someone New

Satchel Paige was about as good as any pitcher in baseball when Joe Nuxhall made his abbreviated debut. But baseball's color barrier kept him out of the major leagues until 1948.

Paige made the best of his late start. He was still pitching in 1965 when he was fifty-nine years (plus 78 days) old. Paige's last game was for the Kansas City Athletics. But he also suited up in 1968 for the Atlanta Braves, who quickly stationed him in a rocking chair on the sidelines. Paige had an official contract to play, too, even if he didn't do so. The Braves were helping him get an extra season in so that he could qualify for a pension.

The minor leagues give baseball even more circumstances to get old-timers into games. Manager Lefty O'Doul, the National League's batting champion in 1929, pinch hit for the Vancouver, B.C., team of the Pacific Coast League in 1956 when he was fifty-nine years old. After fouling off a couple of pitches, O'Doul showed that a good batting eye remains with a great hitter. He lashed a triple. O'Doul was followed to bat by one of his coaches, fifty-one-year-old Eddie Taylor. The "younger" oldster could only manage a single.

The Asheville, N. C., team of the Tri-State League dipped even further into its ranks to come up with a pitcher in a late 1954 game against Knoxville. Asheville summoned its fifty-three-year-old groundskeeper Bud Shaney to the mound. Shaney pitched five innings of shutout ball, giving up just four hits. He also beat out a hit himself. Shaney had retired from professional baseball in 1942 after a 22-year career.

Some of the best youthful performances in big league baseball include:

Al Kaline, of the Detroit Tigers, who won a batting championship in the American League in 1955 when he was only twenty. Kaline had over 200 hits and batted .340 that season. He never did that well again, ironically, in his 23-year career.

Freddie Lindstrom, of the old New York Giants, who participated in a World Series game in 1924 when he was only eighteen years, ten months and thirteen days "old."

Lou Boudreau, of the Cleveland Indians, who took over as manager of his team in 1942 when he was only twenty-four years old. He continued to star as shortstop too, and at age thirty led the Indians to a World Series triumph.

Bobo Holloman, of the St. Louis Browns, who made his first big-league start in 1953 his best one—he pitched a no-hitter against the Philadelphia Athletics. Holloman rarely pitched well after that.

Grover Cleveland Alexander, of the Philadelphia Phillies, who won 28 games in his rookie year, 1911.

George Watkins, of the St. Louis Cardinals, who batted .373 as a rookie in 1930.

Wally Berger, of the Boston Braves in 1930, and *Frank Robinson,* of the Cincinnati Reds in 1956, who each hit 38 homers as rookies.

The Player Who Paid to Get into the Ballpark

Joe Carolan, a twenty-one-year-old Detroiter, had enough confidence in his baseball ability to venture down to Columbus, Ga., in the spring of 1954 to seek a tryout with the minor-league Cardinals of that city.

The burly, 230-pounder got his tryout all right, but not until he paid his way into the ballpark and asked to speak to the Columbus manager.

The manager took one look at Carolan's size and learned about his determination. So he offered to let the Detroiter take batting practice with his team. Carolan knocked three balls out of the park during the drills. The manager responded by offering him a contract.

Carolan played that same day against the Macon team he paid to see play.

On his first time up, in the first inning, Joe Carolan got his first hit as a professional. A grand-slam home run, naturally.

His Second Pro Game—a No-Hitter

Mickey Mattiace got off to a fast start in his first ten days as a professional baseball pitcher. The twenty-year-old New Yorker, pitching for Palatka in the Florida State League, beat Daytona Beach on a no-hitter in his second pro game in April, 1960. He won his next start, then followed it up with another no-hitter against Tampa.

In just ten days as a pro, he had two no-hitters and a third victory.

Before the season was over, Mattiace added two more one-hitters to his impressive portfolio.

A Fast Start for a Teenage Pitcher

It was only an exhibition game, but for pitcher Dick Ellsworth it was a major performance.

The eighteen-year-old Ellsworth had signed a $50,000 bonus pact with the Chicago Cubs in June of 1958. So when the Cubs brought the 6-foot, 4-inch Californian into Chicago for a visit, they decided to have a real look at the strong-arm hurler.

On June 18, Ellsworth was assigned to pitch a mid-season intercity charity game against the Chicago White Sox. Before 22,000 fans at Comiskey Park, Ellsworth mowed down the White Sox on just four hits and beat them 1-0 in his first professional game.

That prompted the Cubs to keep him in the majors for another look. But Ellsworth wasn't so fortunate the second time around. In a regular-season game, he got blasted for four hits and gave up three walks in less than three innings. He lost the game, and was farmed out shortly thereafter.

MISCELLANEOUS

Going Home in Record Time

Man is moving much faster in sports nowadays than he was in 1931. For example, the record for the 100-yard dash in track was then 9.6 seconds; now it's 9.1 and in danger of dipping below 9.0. Yet no man has since circled the bases in baseball faster than Evar Swanson did in '31.

The "Swift Swede" was a 170-pound, all-around sports star, who once won sixteen letters at Lombard (Ill.) College and played four years of professional football as well as making it to the major leagues as an outfielder. Swanson was a pretty good major leaguer, with a lifetime batting average over .300 for 515 games, but he played in an era when the pay was not particularly high. The most Swanson ever made was $8,500.

To compensate, athletes of that time used to go barnstorming in the off-season or take part in special promotions during regular-season games, such as fungo hitting contests, throwing for distance, etc. Getting timed for circling the bases was another favorite—and Swanson's specialty.

Swanson took part in one such promotion during a Cincinnati game on September 15, 1929. His competition included his fleet teammate, Ethan Allen, and the Boston Braves' Lance Richbourg. Each man would have one try, lining up like a sprinter behind home plate and then dashing around the bases, touching each one, before tagging home again. The minimum distance for the run is 120 yards.

Another Cincinnati player, Hans Lobert, had set the big-league record at 13.8 seconds in 1910. Swanson was in the midst of his best major-league season, one in which he would steal 33 bases to finish second in the National League, so he was a top candidate to challenge Lobert's old mark.

With a $75 prize offered by the ballclub, there was even more incentive besides pride.

After Allen and Richbourg made their runs, Swanson went into his trackman's start and waited for the signal to dash off toward first. When he got it, he raced fast and intelligently, careful to tag the inside of each base and not waste extra motion by taking wide turns at the bases.

Stopwatches in 1929 clocked runners to the fifths of a second instead of tenths so Swanson reached home in 13.4, completely smashing the old mark. A later look at the timing device indicated he was closer to 13.3; but the 13.4 stood.

Two years later, on September 20, 1931, the stopwatches were divided into seconds. That year, before a game at Columbus, O., Swanson got his 13.3 officially. The record has never been topped. George Case, a great baserunner for the Washington Senators, came closest, clocking 13.5 in 1943. Mickey Rivers, an outfielder for the California Angels, attempted the feat in 1971 and could do only 14.3 as he rounded the bases. He found out what many fleet candidates did—that it takes more than speed.

"I probably wasn't the fastest player in baseball," Swanson told sportswriter Larry Bortstein years later. "But I knew how to run the bases."

Asked why his record has stood so long, Swanson said, "We did it for pride, but for money, too. With the money these fellows make today, why should they risk anything?"

The Player Who Signed a Big-League Contract
Before He ever Played a Game of Baseball

The Cincinnati Reds were holding a tryout camp in 1947 on one of the wide-open ranges of Texas when a scraggly teenager showed up. The player had never participated in a baseball game before, and at age sixteen hardly seemed like much of a prospect. But the manager of the Bonham, Texas, softball team suggested that his star shortstop, 5-foot, 11-inch, 160-pound Roy McMillan, go over to Tyler, Texas, and attend the Reds' camp.

Tryout camps were fairly open in those days and big-league teams were generous in giving anyone a quick look-see before inviting the outstanding back for more sessions.

They liked what they saw in the youthful McMillan as he scooted around the infield like a waterbug, scooping ground balls out of the dirt and stabbing line drives in the air. McMillan, who would earn the nickname "Radar" in coming years for his ability to trace the baseball in the field, was offered a contract. He was signed for $250.

McMillan began to play almost immediately for the Reds' farm club in Ballinger, Texas, of the Lone Star State League. He moved swiftly up the ranks—to Tyler, Columbia, S. C., and Tulsa, one step each year as his hitting progressed. Fielding was no problem for Radar. McMillan began 1951 in Tulsa, which had a Class AA team, and then was moved up to the majors partway through the same season. He played mostly short but also some second and third base as a rookie. His hitting wasn't much (only .211) but the Reds weren't that concerned.

In fact, before they were more than a few games into the 1952 season, the Reds traded away their 1951 starting shortstop, Virgil Stallcup, and installed McMillan in the position. McMillan started every game for the Reds in 1952.

The fact that Stallcup had been the National League's leading shortstop in fielding and a .251 hitter showed what the Reds thought of their fledgling twenty-one-year-old prospect who was still learning the game.

The Reds stayed with McMillan despite a rocky start at bat in which he got only two hits in 52. He justified their confidence by winding up the season a decent .244 hitter who, lacking size, still placed enough good hits to finish second on the team in runs batted in.

Typical of the play that kept him in the majors in those early years was a doubleheader in early 1952 against the Philadelphia Phillies.

In the first game, McMillan snared a line drive off hard-hitting Smokey Burgess, who could only shake his head in disbelief. Later McMillan dug a slow roller out of the ground and threw long and hard to first base to beat out speedy Granny Hamner. McMillan was off balance when he threw.

In the second game, McMillan hit his first home run of the year. His next heroics were in the field. Radar got a grounder in back of second base and tossed out Richie Ashburn, one of the fastest men in baseball, before he got to first. McMillan made the grab and the throw in one motion.

Thus in less than six years after he played his first game of baseball, Roy McMillan was the best shortstop in the majors.

McMillan lasted for 16 years in the majors, playing over 2,000 games at shortstop for the Reds, the Milwaukee Braves and the New York Mets.

Another player reached the major leagues in 1951—the same year as McMillan did—and shared the distinction of getting a big-league contract before he played his first baseball game.

But the circumstances were different for Eddie Gaedel.

Gaedel, who couldn't field a lick and never got the

bat off his shoulder in his only appearance to the plate, was banned from baseball after just one at-bat. He was a midget, 43 inches (3 feet, 7 inches) "tall."

Gaedel's appearance for the St. Louis Browns in an official American League game against the Detroit Tigers on August 19, 1951, was something of a gimmick. When Gaedel waddled out of the Browns' dugout during the second game of a doubleheader between two teams going nowhere in the pennant race, umpire Ed Hurley challenged him. A man has to have a *bona fide* professional baseball contract, filed with the commissioner's office, before he can participate in a big-league game.

Gaedel reached into a pocket of his tailor-made Brown uniform, which bore the number "⅛", and showed Hurley what he didn't want to see—an official contract okayed by the major league office. Since it had been late in the season when several teams were bringing up unknown minor-league prospects, Gaedel's name was okayed at the commissioner's desk without a challenge. The whole event had been staged by Browns' owner Bill Veeck, as humorous an impressario as baseball has ever known. Veeck guarded his secret from just about everyone, including the people in his own organization.

He had hired Gaedel out of a circus and instructed him under threat of his life not to swing at any pitches once he got to bat against the Tigers.

The Tiger pitcher, Bob Cain, was so stunned in trying to put a ball into Gaedel's miniscule strike zone that he finally got down on his knees and pitched to the midget. But it was all in vain for Cain. Gaedel drew four straight balls and waddled down to first base, where he was quickly replaced with a pinch runner. Veeck had had his fun and just about everybody but the commissioner's office had a good laugh.

Eddie Gaedel, who had never played a game of baseball, made his debut at the top. He and Roy McMillan probably are the only men in the twentieth century to receive a contract with a major-league club before playing a baseball game.

The next day, twenty-six-year-old Eddie Gaedel was banned from baseball—the last man to suffer such a fate at the big-league level.

Covington Played for 21 Different Teams

Chester Covington was a late starter in professional baseball. He didn't pitch for money until he was twenty-eight. Seems that his other interests—he was a pro boxer, a patent medicine salesman, a railroad worker and a wrestling referee, among other things—absorbed his time until 1939 when he inked his first minor-league baseball contract.

If Covington had been a man on the move before he joined the Portsmouth, Va., team, it was nothing compared to the way he zigzagged through organized baseball. Covington played for a total of 21 different teams in the 12 years that were to follow his late debut. Counting repeat performances in some minor-league towns he returned to—including Tampa two more times—Covington had 24 different assignments during his dozen years.

A rugged 225-pound lefthander, who had a 187-19-10 record as a boxer, Covington used to say he liked to train on "franks and beers." However he trained, he trained well. He had a total of 219 victories during his professional baseball career.

Though he joked around, he was no clown on the field. Two years after he signed his first contract, he ran up a 14-game winning streak. Two years later, in 1943, he was named Minor League Player of the Year for his performance with Scranton, Pa., of the Eastern League. Scranton was the tenth team Covington played for, so by then he had an opportunity to get some revenge on some of the teams that discarded him. In one of those moments, he tossed a perfect game against Springfield, Mass., with whom he had played a couple of years before. He stretched his string to 16⅔ hitless and 45 scoreless innings.

The good 1943 season earned Covington a trip to the majors for 1944. He pitched briefly, splitting a pair of decisions for the Philadelphia Phillies and getting thoroughly disgusted with management when he was forced to walk Stan Musial intentionally in one game.

Before the season was over, Covington was back in the minors with Utica, N.Y., to continue his minor-league odyssey. He was thirty-four at the time, but some of his best pitching was ahead of him.

Covington pitched for the Tampa Smokers in 1946 and displayed some remarkable control by walking only 55 men in 303 innings. In 1950, at age thirty-nine, he won 18 games for a second-division Fort Lauderdale club.

After that stopover, Covington moved to Tampa for the third time, then Lakeland, Fla. Lakeland dealt him to Sanford in the Florida State League. But for once, Covington declined an assignment. He joined the Greensboro team instead and posted a part-time 9-1 record, not bad for a forty-year-old.

In all, and in order, Covington pitched for Portsmouth, Tarboro N.C., Goldsboro N.C., Hollywood Fla., Fort Pierce Fla., Springfield, Jacksonville Fla., Birmingham, Louisville, Scranton, the Philadelphia Phillies, Utica, Chattanooga, Tampa, Montgomery, Miami, Port Chester N.Y., Portsmouth again, Tampa again, Palatka Fla., Fort Lauderdale, Tampa again, Lakeland and Greensboro.

Even more traveled around the baseball circuit was Louis (Bobo) Newsom, the lovable loser who spent 25 years shuttling in and out of baseball cities, mostly in the majors.

Newsom pitched for "only" 18 different teams. But consider this. He was traded or sold to the Washington Senators four different times, the St. Louis Browns three times, and returned to the Brooklyn Dodgers—his initial big-league club in 1929—13 years later. Bobo played for nine different major-league teams. In addition to the above, he also toiled for New York, Detroit, Boston and Philadelphia in the American League and New York and Chicago in the National. He was involved in trades that totaled 19 players.

He was released outright by five different clubs in his latter years and yet each time he hooked up with another big-league club.

A 6-foot 3-inch, 205-pounder, Newsom left some remarkable marks for losers to shoot for. He is, for instance, the only twentieth century 200-game winner to lose more than he won (211-222). He led the American League in losses a total of four times, a record. In 1938, he set a major-league record by giving up the most earned runs in a season—186—but still posted a 20-16 record for the St. Louis Browns.

But he probably reached his "peak" on September 18, 1934, when he pitched nine hitless innings for the Browns—but lost to the Boston Red Sox in the tenth inning!

Bobo Newsom probably would have been proud of Ted Gray, a fellow American League pitcher who hung around for nine years in the majors despite a losing record (59-74). In the lefthander's final season, 1955, Gray tied a big-league record by playing for four teams in the same season.

Gray did it the easy way: he played two games for the Chicago White Sox, two for the Cleveland

Indians, one for the New York Yankees and finally nine for the Baltimore Orioles before calling it a career. That gave him four teams in just 19 games in one season—a tough act to follow. In all, he pitched only 23 innings.

The One-Armed Major-League Outfielder

The talent in major-league baseball was thin in 1945. The more athletic Americans were overseas, trying to wind down World War II. Perhaps only in such an era could the big-league ranks include a one-armed outfielder. But for that one season, such a man earned publicity that would have made some Hall of Famers envious.

Pete (One-Arm) Gray was his name. And if the gutsy, little man was an oddity for the big leagues, he wasn't odd as a ballplayer. He came up through the minor leagues legitimately, and he stayed with the St. Louis Browns of the American League for a whole pennant-chasing season. Gray was good enough to be in a total of 77 major-league games that year, and more often than not he was entrusted to take an outfield position.

"He's no side-show freak," maintained the Browns manager, Luke Sewell. "He's a fine player, fast, courageous, and he can hit. We use him when he can help us win, the same as any two-armed player."

Born Peter J. Wyshner, he lost his arm at the age of six, when he fell off a truck and got it caught in the spokes of a wheel. When he had healed, he refused to let himself be denied sports. He played football, softball, basketball, hockey and other sports that were popular in the coal-mining town of Nanticoke, Pa. He put in such long hours at his games, especially baseball, that his father would end up delivering sandwiches to the playground to ensure that the boy got some nourishment. For hours, Pete would go off on his own and practice. He used to toss up rocks and hit them with a stick down near the railroad yards. Before long, the wrist on his left hand became very powerful.

Young Wyshner changed his name to Pete Gray after his brother adopted that last name during a prizefighting career. Then Pete Gray set out to make a living professionally in sports, too. His hard work paid off for him by the time he was sixteen. Though he didn't play high-school baseball, he was better than the other sandlotters in the coal-mining area. He was confident, too.

In 1939, Pete went to the World's Fair in New York City. He brought his glove along, because he had heard that baseball tryouts were being held in Brooklyn. Pete didn't connect with any team that year, but three seasons later, at age twenty-five, he hooked up with the Three Rivers, Ont., team in the Canadian-American League. Despite a broken collarbone in his debut, Gray made a comeback and batted .381.

Quickly he was promoted to the classy Memphis Chicks team of the Southern Association. He began to make a name for himself, hitting .289 in 1943 and .333 the following year. During that banner 1944 campaign, Pete was a terror on the basepaths, stealing 68 times (including 10 thefts of home plate).

For those who figured his one arm would prove to be too much of a handicap in the outfield, Pete had a surprise. He fielded well, catching the ball in his specially made glove with no padding, then quickly tucking the glove under the stump of his right arm, digging out the ball and throwing it—all in one effortless motion. In one game, Pete made an unassisted double play from centerfield.

At the end of the 1944 season, 14 of the Southern Association's top sportswriters sent in their ballots for the league's Most Valuable Player. Gray's name topped the list on 12 of them.

The St. Louis Browns, who had just won the

American League pennant, paid Memphis $20,-000 for Gray's contract and offered the amazing one-armed player an opportunity to make the big leagues.

The Browns were paying for talent, but they soon found out they had acquired a drawing card, too. At a time when baseball was suffering from wartime doldrums, huge crowds flocked to see Pete Gray wherever he traveled in the American League. Once 65,000 turned out to see him play at Cleveland. Pete treated the curiosity seekers to a triple on his first time up. A like number of fans were expected to see him play for the first time at Yankee Stadium, but a bad-weather forecast dampened the enthusiasm. Still, 40,000 fans braved the weather. Pete was giving the big leagues a much-needed shot in the arm.

The Brown often took advantage of Gray's appeal. In the Yankee Stadium debut, Manager Sewell purposely held him back during the pre-game introduction of the Brown players. When Pete finally took the field, he got a standing ovation.

His popularity caused some alarm among teammates, who were envious of his unintentional wooing of the crowds. They sometimes felt he was put in games ahead of better players just to satisfy the fans. And umpires were perturbed that Gray could do no wrong in the eyes of the crowds, whether they were Brown fans or not.

But for the season, Gray often held his own, playing against such standouts as Bobby Feller and Hal Newhouser.

He earned most of his plaudits.

After a slow start typical of many rookies, in which he had only a drag bunt hit to show for 13 at-bats, Gray went 4-for-9 and scored three runs in two games during spring training. That, coupled with his flawless fielding (10 putouts, one assist, no errors in five games) enabled him to make the Brown team.

Once the regular season began, the twenty-eight-year-old rookie proved he was big-league caliber even though he was no day-to-day star. In an important series with the New York Yankees early in the season, Pete displayed his prowess both at bat and in the field. He singled twice in the first inning of a crucial doubleheader and was the focal point of a Brown rally for seven runs. He singled again in the third and drove in a run in the fifth as the Browns won the opener, 10-1. During that same game, he went back to the leftfield wall for important putouts, one with the bases loaded and two outs.

In the nightcap, Gray walked, singled and also came within a halfstep of beating out a drag bunt. In the outfield, he made six putouts, including a line-drive catch that he snared below his knees while on a dead run. The Browns won that game, too. A crowd of more than 20,000 showered him with applause all afternoon.

Later in the season, during a July 4 twin bill against the Philadelphia A's, Gray's 32-ounce bat exploded again. He slugged a long double and two singles against the A's best pitcher and drove in the winning runs in the process.

Pete's play inspired the St. Louis *Post-Dispatch*'s baseball writer, J. Roy Stockton, to write, "It was a great exhibition of courage and you can use that word without restraint or blush, even in these war-torn days, when you sing of a gamester like Peter Gray."

Gray got into 77 games during the season, mostly as a regular outfielder. Crowds poured into once-empty stadiums even when it was unlikely that he would play. Sometimes, his appearances—demanded by the curious fans—worked against the Browns' efforts to defend their American League title. In a game against the Yankees, for example, the Browns had an 8-2 lead in the last of the seventh inning, so Manager Sewell decided to treat the 40,000-strong crowd to a look at Gray. Pete fumbled a single during a Yankee rally and the Browns subsequently lost the game in extra innings—and also the second game of the double-header. The Browns never did recover from that twin loss and finished in third place.

For the season, Pete only batted .218. That, coupled with the return of baseball veterans from the war in 1946, shortened Gray's big-league career. In November, 1945, his contract was sold to Toledo of the American Association.

Even Pete admitted, "The pitching is a little bit too tough for me up there (in the majors)."

He shipped out to Toledo for 1946, dropped a few notches on the minor-league scale to Elmira, N.Y., for 1948, then moved upward again to Dallas in 1949 before finally retiring. But the stint in the majors earned Pete his share of immortality, to say nothing of a little extra cash. Parlaying his fame in the off-season one fall, he earned $5400 on a short barnstorming tour.

Pete Gray wasn't the only one-armed player to compete at the major-league level. On September 13, 1883, Hugh Dailey of the Cleveland team in the National League hurled a no-hitter against the Philadelphia ballclub and came out a 1-0 winner. "One-Arm" Dailey also pitched 18 other shutouts during his big-league career with eight teams in the 1880s, and totaled 74 victories in all.

Pete Gray's Professional Baseball Record

Batting

Year	Team	G	AB	R	H	2B	3B	HR	SB	BB	SO	RBI	Pct
1942	Three Rivers	42	160	31	61	5	0	0	5	14	3	13	.381
1943	Memphis	126	453	56	131	7	6	0	13	19	11	42	.289
1944	Memphis	129	501	119	167	21	9	5	68	44	12	60	.333
1945	St. Louis	77	234	26	51	6	2	0	5	13	11	13	.218
1946	Toledo	48	96	14	24	3	0	0	2	5	0	7	.250
1948	Elmira	82	269	37	78	7	2	0	5	16	6	14	.290
1949	Dallas	45	56	18	12	2	0	0	5	1	1	5	.214

Fielding

Year	Team	G	PO	A	E	DP	Pct
1942	Three Rivers	41	111	1	1	1	.991
1943	Memphis	122	312	3	8	1	.975
1944	Memphis	129	336	5	6	0	.983
1945	St. Louis	61	162	3	7	1	.959
1946	Toledo	30	49	0	4	0	.925
1948	Elmira	70	120	2	6	1	.953
							1.000

The Miracle Inning

Things didn't look good for the American League Philadelphia Athletics in the fourth game of the 1929 World Series. The National League Chicago Cubs had scored two runs in the fourth inning, five in the sixth and another in the seventh to put the A's behind, 8-0, that October 12 afternoon.

Considering that the game was unfolding in front of the Athletics' own fans in Philadelphia, it was even more embarrassing. The chances of the A's catching up were lessened by Charlie Root's pitching. He had held the A's in check with a mere three hits going into the bottom of the seventh inning.

The Athletics' venerable 67-year-old manager, Connie Mack, had already gone through three of his pitchers in what seemed a hopeless contest. Just before the seventh inning got under way, he considered pulling some of his other regulars to rest them for the next game. But when Al Sim-

mons opened the Athletics' half of the inning
with a homer, for which he got a guarded applause from the fans, and Jimmie Foxx followed
with a single, Mack reconsidered. He was right;
the A's collected three more singles and were now
down only 8-3.

A pinch hitter for pitcher popped out, but second baseman Max Bishop singled to drive in the
fourth run and suddenly the fans were cheering
up.

With the crowd on the edge of the seats, centerfielder Mule Haas pumped a fly ball to the outfield. It should have been an out, but the Cubs'
Hack Wilson lost it when he was blinded by the
sun. As the ball rolled into deep centerfield with
the confused Wilson in pursuit, two runners made
it home and Haas himself was rounding the bases
with abandon. He too scored on an inside-the-
park homer. The score was now 8-7, with just
one out.

Meanwhile, Cub Manager Joe McCarthy was
shuttling pitchers in and out of the game, to no
avail.

Catcher Mickey Cochrane walked. Then Simmons and Foxx, with their second hits of the inning, drove him home to tie the score. McCarthy
brought in his fourth pitcher, but A's rightfielder
Bing Miller got to base when hit by a pitched
ball, and Jimmy Dykes, collecting his second hit,
scored two men with a double.

In only nine World Series games up to that time had a team scored as many as 10 runs in a game. The A's now had 10 in an inning, a record that would hold for years until tied by the 1968 Detroit Tigers. After three quarters of a century of World Series action, no one has bettered the mark for hits.

Oddly, the next out came when Mack sent another pinch hitter to bat, and another strikeout brought the amazing inning to an end.

With the victory within reach, Mack decided to go with his ace pitcher, Lefty Grove, for the final two innings. Grove proved to be a good choice as he blanked the Cubs for the save. The Athletics won the game, 10-8.

Two days later, the A's finished off the Cubs and won the series, five games to one.

Scoring after the Last Out

On May 28, 1922, a 2-1 duel between the New York Yankees and the St. Louis Browns seemed to be over, with the powerful Yankees winning as usual. Yank pitcher Sam Jones, who had been hit freely but fruitlessly by the Browns, retired the first two Browns to face him in the ninth inning before an overflow, boisterous crowd in New York. Two Browns reached base with singles. Jones was headed toward first to cover that base after the next man, John Tobin, hit a slow roller to the first baseman. The Brown baserunner who had been on second base went all the way home. As Jones took the underhand throw, the fans spilled onto the field and chased the players to their dressing rooms.

But then the umpire reversed himself and ruled that Jones had juggled the catch at first base, making Tobin safe, and making the score 2-all in the unfinished game.

Within fifteen minutes, the players were recalled to the field, the diamond was cleaned up and the fans were back in the stands. One player was summoned out of the shower.

Tobin, who had scored the Browns' only other run in the eighth inning when the Yankees had a 2-0 lead, went to first base.

From then on in, what should have been a routine victory for the Yanks, who were winning regularly despite the suspension of Babe Ruth, turned into a nightmare.

The first man up when play resumed singled, driving in the go-ahead run for the Browns. The next batter was walked intentionally to fill the bases, but the Yankees were getting madder and madder by the moment. Particularly the pitcher.

He walked the next man to force Tobin in.

Then a Brown cleaned the bases with a home run.

And Urb Shocker, the ace of the St. Louis staff, put the embarrassed Yanks down in order in the bottom of the ninth.

The Browns had scored seven runs on the Yanks after the "last out." They held an 8-2 lead at a time when they should have been en route back to their hotel to moan a defeat.

The game was significant for the upstart Browns, who weren't considered in the same class with the Yankees. St. Louis battled the New Yorkers down to the final game before losing the pennant that season.

No Sweat

It was hot at Chicago's Wrigley Field on August 24, 1922, but no one was affected more than Cubs Manager Bill Killefer. A 200-pounder in his second year of managing, Killefer had watched his team score 25 runs in the first four innings—and then *nearly blow the game*!

The game that day with the Philadelphia Phillies was bizarre almost from the start. The Cubs scored in their bottom half of the first but went behind, 3-1, in the second. Then they sent 13 men to bat in the second to win back the lead. During the rally, Bob O'Farrell homered and got another hit to spark his team to 10 runs.

The Phillies fought back, climbing all over the Cubs until they cut the margin to 11-6 after three and a half innings.

But again the Cubs rallied, this time sending 19 men to bat in the bottom of the fourth. Fourteen of those men scored to give the Cubs a 25-6 lead.

The game Phillies got back three more runs in the next inning, but their hopes for a victory that day seemed unrealistic.

The Cubs got another run, then the two teams settled back for their first scoreless inning in the seventh.

But then Killefer's enjoyment of the slugfest came to an end.

The Phillies, however, rallied for eight runs in the top of the eighth and began tearing into the Cubs in the ninth. The first batter singled, the second walked, the third singled and the fourth doubled. And Killefer sweated.

He had reason to.

After the Phils scored three runs, Killefer changed pitchers and brought 215-pound rookie Tiny Osborne into the game. Osborne struck out the first Phil to face him but gave up a run, and later two more. In between he got a strike out.

With the score at 26-23, the two teams had already scored more runs than any two teams during a game in major-league history (before or since) and the bases were still loaded. Coming to bat was Bevo LeBourveau, a pretty good hitter.

But Osborne got him, too, on a strikeout—the third of the inning. That saved the day for Killefer. But the pyrotechnics, in which two teams made a record 51 hits (six more than any other two teams) in a nine-inning game, cost him dearly. Killefer sweated away six pounds during the game, mostly in the final two innings.

An Unusual Twinbill in the Majors

When the Milwaukee Braves prepared for a doubleheader on September 24, 1954, the scouting report before the game was bigger than usual. That day the Braves would have to play two different teams.

It happened this way:

Two days earlier, the Braves had met the Cincinaati Reds for what seemed to be the final match between the two teams during the regular season. The Braves won, 3-1, but the Reds protested a play.

The Reds had been trailing 3-1 in the ninth inning with one out and runners on first and third. Cincy's Bob Borkowski struck out, but the ball eluded Braves catcher Del Crandall so Borkowski dashed to first.

Meanwhile, Crandall threw to third baseman Eddie Mathews, who missed a tag on Gus Bell and quickly tossed to first to try to get Borkow-ski. The ball hit the base runner on the back and bounced into rightfield. Two runners scored. But after a 15-minute dispute, the Braves were awarded the victory.

Then National League President Warren Giles upheld Cincinnati's protest. With the season coming to a close and the Braves involved in the pennant race, Cincinnati was ordered to go back to Miïwaukee for the finish of the disputed game. The game was replayed with Bell at third and a man at second, which was consistent with Giles' ruling. The score was held at 3-1, Milwaukee's favor, and two outs.

Cincinnati got two runs in after the game was started and again tied the score at 3-all. But the Braves scored in the bottom of the ninth and won, 4-3.

Meanwhile, the St. Louis Cardinals were watching all this and awaiting their own previously scheduled September 24 date with the Braves.

The Braves took that contest, too, by a 4-2 score.

It was all academic, though. Not the Braves, or the Cards, or the Reds got close to going to the World Series.

The 26-Inning Game

It rained in Boston on the morning of May 1, 1920. What players and fans had hoped would be a sunny May Day dampened their enthusiasm for the scheduled 3 o'clock game between the home-town Braves and the visiting Brooklyn Dodgers. The players had to show up, however, when it was announced the game would be played as scheduled. A small crowd of 2,000 turned out.

Too bad. The pitchers, Brooklyn's Leon Cadore and Boston's Joe Oeschger, had staged an 11-inning, 1-0 duel when they met two weeks beforehand. The Dodgers won that one.

But it was too bad for other reasons, too. For Cadore and Oeschger were about to turn in one of the greatest "iron men" feats on record.

The game began rather routinely, with neither team scoring until the fifth inning. Then the Dodgers scored first again, when Cadore advanced a runner into scoring position with a fielder's choice play and Ivan Olson singled the man home.

The Braves tied the score in the sixth inning after Wally Cruise tripled with one man out, and scored on a single. Actually, the Dodgers could have nailed Cruise when he took off for home after a short fly to leftfield. Brooklyn's Zack Wheat made a shoestring catch of the ball and tried to double Cruise, who had run halfway to the plate. But there was no one on third to take the throw. Cruise scampered back safely and later scored on the single.

It was the end of the scoring—but hardly the end of the game. For 20 more innings, one goose egg after another was entered into the box score. Two baseball teams played exceedingly tight defense and refused to allow a run.

There were a few threats, like the Braves' rally in the ninth when they filled the bases only to get caught in a double play. The Dodgers made a bid to win in the seventeenth inning only to see an amazing double play (pitcher to catcher to first to catcher) stymie the rally. The throw to first had not been on time but the first baseman, Walt Holke, got it home in time to stop the would-be scorer. It was Holke's only assist of the day but next to the pitchers, he got the biggest workout that May Day. He made a total of 42 putouts at first, and didn't have an error.

The real heroes, however, were pitchers

Oeschger of Boston and Cadore of Brooklyn. They went all the way—26 innings in baseball's longest game, inning-wise.

Oeschger gave up just nine hits in pitching the equivalent of nearly three full games. Cadore gave up only 15 hits. They each struck out just seven men, but they walked only nine players between them.

Oeschger had gotten the Sunday starting assignment because his manager, George Stallings, was a superstitious type who figured his religious, church-going righthander might get a few breaks from the Man Upstairs if he pitched on the Sabbath. As it turned out, the Man was treating everybody the same—very evenly, to be sure—that May 1 in 1920. After 26 innings—spanning 3 hours and 50 minutes—of baseball, the game was called.

The players were begging for an additional inning. They wanted to be able to say that they had played three full games within one. But it was getting too dark to continue. Umpire Barry McCormick told them they'd have to wear miners' lamps on their baseball caps if they wanted to go on.

Pitcher Cadore was one of the biggest protesters. But after the game was called, he justified the umpire's decision when he went home and slept for 36 straight hours. Meanwhile, Oeschger had to contend with stories in Boston papers

The 26-Inning Marathon

Dodgers	AB	R	H	PO	A	E
Ivy Olson, 2b	10	0	1	5	8	1
Bernie Neis, rf	10	0	1	9	0	0
Jimmy Johnston, 3b	10	0	2	3	1	0
Zach Wheat, lf	9	0	2	3	0	0
Hi Myers, cf	2	0	1	3	2	0
Wally Hood, cf	6	0	0	9	1	0
Ed Konetchy, 1b	9	0	1	30	0	0
Chuck Ward, ss	10	0	0	5	3	1
Ernie Krueger, c	2	1	0	4	3	0
Rowdy Elliott, c	7	0	0	7	3	0
Leon Cadore, p	10	0	0	1	12	0
Totals	85	1	9	78	31	2

Braves	AB	R	H	PO	A	E
Ray Powell, cf	7	0	1	8	0	1
Charley Pick, 2b	11	0	0	6	11	2
Leslie Mann, lf	10	0	2	6	0	0
Walton Cruise, rf	9	1	1	4	0	0
Walter Holke, 1b	10	0	2	42	1	0
Tony Boeckel, 3b	11	0	3	1	7	0
Rabbit Maranville, ss	10	0	3	1	9	0
Mickey O'Neil, c	2	0	0	4	1	0
a-Lloyd Christenbury	1	0	1	0	0	0
Hank Gowdy, c	6	0	1	6	0	0
Joe Oeschger, p	9	0	1	0	11	0
Totals	86	1	15	78	41	2

```
Dodgers ......... 000 010 000 000 000 000 000 00—1
Braves .......... 000 001 000 000 000 000 000 00—1
```

a-Singled for O'Neil in ninth. Runs batted in—Olson, Boeckel. Two-base hits—Maranville, Oescher. Three-base hit—Cruise. Stolen bases—Myers, Hood. Sacrifices—Hood, Oeschger, Powell, O'Neil, Holke, Cruise. Double plays—Olson and Konetchy; Oeschger, Holke and Gowdy. Bases on balls—Off Cadore 5, off Oeschger 4. Struck out—By Cadore 7, by Oeschger 7. Wild pitch—Oeschger. Left on bases —Dodgers 11, Braves 16. Umpires—McCormick and Hart. Time of game—3 hours, 50 minutes.

that his career was probably ruined by the 26-inning marathon. He squelched that talk by pitching, and winning, eight days later.

The game was finally played off on June 25, with the Braves winning. But the finish has been obscured by history. What was historically important was a pitching duel and a tight defense on baseball's longest day.

There have been games that took more time than the 26-inning no-contest between the Braves and the Dodgers. Marathon games of more than six-and-a-half hours have been played in the majors, particularly in the 1960s. For short-term games, one must go back into history. The New York Giants beat the Philadelphia Phillies, 6-1, in a 51-minute nine-inning game in 1919.

But the real quickie must have been the showdown on August 30, 1916, between the Asheville and Winston-Salem teams in the North Carolina League.

The minor leaguers were playing an unimportant late-season contest that day, and since they traveled by train the visiting Winston-Salem manager requested a fast match. The starting time of the game was moved up from 2 P.M. to 1:28. By 1:59—31 minutes later—the two teams had their nine innings in.

The hitters swung at everything that was pitched and tried particularly to connect on first pitches. The teams raced to the field when their side was out and on one occasion they almost resumed play without a catcher. The game moved along so fast that the regular umpire was stunned to learn that four innings had passed by the time he arrived on the scene for the scheduled 2 o'clock starting time.

Somehow the teams found the time to score three runs between them. Winston-Salem won the game, 2-1, before dashing off to catch the 3'clock train.

The College World Serious

College baseball in the United States has had a World Series of its own since 1947, and the tournament has gotten even more competitive in recent times. Nowadays more young players prefer college baseball to toiling in the minor leagues in their quests to reach the majors.

In the first 25 years of the College World Series, only one team (Texas) ever won two championships in a row. Thus the comment made by Southern Cal's freshman first baseman Daryl Arenstein didn't attract too much attention in 1970. Arenstein was celebrating the winning of the 1970 title with his Trojan teammates when he predicted that it would be the first of four straight such titles for him.

Arenstein continued to hold down the starting first baseman's job for the Trojans throughout his four college years and Southern Cal continued to win titles. In 1973, Arenstein and USC got their fourth straight when they topped Arizona State, 4-3, in the final game at Omaha, Nebraska.

Even Arenstein, however, had to admit that his prediction four years earlier had not been too rational a statement. "It sounded like the right thing to say then," he admitted in 1973. Still, it will be difficult to match his feat of starting for the winning team in the College World Series four years in a row.

Arenstein's coach, Rod Dedeaux, got a chance to top his protégé in 1974 when he guided Southern Cal to yet another title. A millionaire in the construction business, Dedeaux worked virtually for nothing as coach. It was reported that he got only one dollar a year from the Trojans at his request. But he gave them the most for their money—five straight World Series titles and nine overall since 1958.

Streaking to Nowhere

Early in the season, tough-minded John McGraw felt that his 1916 New York Giants were spending too much effort trying to break the major-league record of 19 straight victories. So he tore up his club halfway through the campaign. Despite the fact that the Giants had won 17 straight and had come close to matching the 19 in a row racked up by the 1906 Chicago White Sox, McGraw didn't hesitate when the streak came to an end and the team slumped into playing .500 ball. He discarded two of his best veterans and demoted his catcher. McGraw was that way: today's game was more important than yesterday's history.

Gone would be Larry Doyle, one of the finest second basemen McGraw ever had, and Bill McKechnie, a competent third baseman. McGraw brought in Buck Herzog for second and Heinie Zimmerman for third. He also acquired Lew McCarthy from the league-leading Brooklyn Dodgers to handle the catching when he became disenchanted with the incumbents at that position. Herzog, Zimmerman and McCarthy were all major-league veterans.

The Giants weren't about to catch the high-flying Dodgers but the fearful McGraw apparently affected them with his wholesale shakeup of the ballclub.

After the Giants split a doubleheader with the Dodgers on September 6, losing the second game, little Ferdie Schupp, a rookie McGraw wanted to see more of, tossed a two-hitter against the Dodgers. He won the game, 4-1. The next day, Jeff Tesreau outdueled the great Grover Cleveland Alexander of the Philadelphia Phillies.

Giant fans began coming alive now that their new-look team was pulling together. In fact, 35,-000 of them showed up for a September 9 doubleheader—the largest crowd up to that time to witness a game at the Polo Grounds.

Pol Perritt gave the throng something more to cheer about. Pitching both ends of the doubleheader against the Phillies, Perritt gave up only eight hits and one run. He collected a pair of 3-1 and 3-0 triumphs for his iron-man efforts.

After a day off, the Giants continued to win day in and day out. They beat the Phillies again and swept four straight games from the Cincinnati Reds.

With Schupp, Tesreau and Rube Benton pitching magnificently, McCarthy hitting nearly

.400 and the new infielders blending in, the Giants became unstoppable. There was a temporary snag after they won 12 straight games. On September 18, after they beat the Pittsburgh Pirates in the first half of a doubleheader, the second game was called in the ninth inning because of darkness. The Giants and Pirates were tied 1-1 at the time. But ties don't figure in winning streaks.

The Giants picked up where they left off by sweeping the Pirates in another doubleheader the next day. Then Schupp, with just a day's rest, defeated the Chicago Cubs, 4-2.

With the season coming to a close and the Giants going nowhere in the standings, it suddenly dawned upon them that they were going to get a second chance at matching the White Sox' record of 19 straight victories.

Slim Salee, a curveball artist who had missed several weeks of action due to illness, came off the sick list to pitch the Giants to their 17th straight when he blanked the Chicago Cubs. Then the Giants matched the White Sox major league record of 19 with a sweep of the St. Louis Cardinals on September 23.

The rash of late-season doubleheaders seemed to increase the probability of defeat. But not for the Giants, who were breathing new life into a lost season. After a day off, they swept the Cards in yet another twinbill. It was their seventh dou-

bleheader in September, and they had only the tie
with the Pirates to mar their slate.

The Cards came close to snapping the streak at
22 games when they took a 2-0 lead into the
ninth inning. But the Giants came back to tie
the game and win it in the tenth on Zimmerman's
base running. Zimmerman opened the tenth with
a single, moved to second and third on back-to-
back bunts, then scored on a wild pitch.

Next came the Boston Braves. Tesreau and
Schupp teamed up in a doubleheader to sweep the
Braves as each recorded his sixth pitching victory
of the streak which had now reached 25 games. A
rainout the following day forced the weary Giants
into another doubleheader with the Braves.

Rube Benton became the third Giant pitcher
to reach six victories during the streak in the
opening game on September 30. And he pitched
better than any Giant yet. Benton faced only
28 batters as he won, 4-0. A single by Jim Konetchy ruined Benton's hopes for a perfect game.

The Giants had now won 26 straight games—
nine of them by shutouts. Only five times had an
opponent come as close as one run. They had won
seven doubleheaders.

Rest was a premium the Giants had forgotten
about. Between September 7, when the streak began, and September 30, they had only three Sun-
days off and were rained out two other days in
which they had to come right back and make up

games. They had beaten every team in the league and shut out all of them except the Dodgers at least once.

But in the second game of the September 30 doubleheader, luck ran out. The Braves crushed the Giants, 8-3.

No team has come close to matching the Giant streak of 26 in that 1916 season. The 1935 Chicago Cubs strung together 21 games in a pennant-winning year. The 1947 New York Yankees won 19.

To add a fillip to their record, the Giants had won all 26 games at home—a feat almost impossible to match. (In their original streak that year, they had won all 17 games on the road.)

Yet for all their efforts, the 1916 Giants could finish no better than fourth place, seven games behind the league-leading Brooklyn Dodgers.

26 Consecutive Victories

September 7	New York 4	Brooklyn	1
September 8	New York 9	Philadelphia	3
September 9	New York 3	Philadelphia	1
	New York 3	Philadelphia	0
September 10	Not scheduled		
September 11	New York 9	Philadelphia	4
September 12	New York 3	Cincinnati	2
September 13	New York 3	Cincinnati	0
	New York 6	Cincinnati	4
September 14	New York 3	Cincinnati	1
September 15	Rained out		
September 16	New York 8	Pittsburgh	2
	New York 4	Pittsburgh	3
September 17	Not scheduled		
September 18	New York 2	Pittsburgh	0
	New York 1	Pittsburgh	1
	(Called in 9th)		
September 19	New York 9	Pittsburgh	2
	New York 5	Pittsburgh	1
September 20	New York 4	Chicago	2
September 21	New York 4	Chicago	0
September 22	New York 5	Chicago	0
September 23	New York 6	St. Louis	1
	New York 3	St. Louis	0
September 24	Not scheduled		
September 25	New York 1	St. Louis	0
	New York 6	St. Louis	2
September 26	New York 6	St. Louis	1
September 27	New York 3	St. Louis	2
September 28	New York 2	Boston	1
	New York 6	Boston	0
September 29	Rained out		
September 30	New York 4	Boston	0

Miscellaneous

Notable Twentieth-Century Win Streaks

1903	Pittsburgh Pirates	15
1904	New York Giants	18
1906	Chicago White Sox	19
1906	New York Yankees	15
1907	New York Giants	17
1909	Pittsburgh Pirates	16
1912	Washington Senators	17
1912	New York Giants	16
1913	Philadelphia A's	15
1916	New York Giants	17
1916	New York Giants	26*
1924	Brooklyn Dodgers	15
1926	New York Yankees	16
1931	Philadelphia A's	17
1935	Chicago Cubs	21
1936	Chicago Cubs	15
1936	New York Giants	15
1946	Boston Red Sox	15
1947	New York Yankees	19
1951	New York Giants	16
1953	New York Giants	18
1960	New York Yankees	15

* Record.